"I've wished frequently that there was a book I could recommend which contained all the information Matthew Hutton has assembled here with such accessible wisdom. His own professional background as a solicitor and tax advisor is evident, but it's his pastoral experience as a priest which has animated this project and taken it into areas we tend to avoid. I thought initially this was a book to commend to others, but now I realize that I needed to read it for myself and to act on it. Your Last Gift will be a blessing to many."

The Rt Revd Graham James - former Bishop of Norwich

"This Book is an essential guide to surviving the administrative burden of grief. Matthew provides us with a sensible and practical approach for preparing for the inevitable with helpful signposts to guide you along the way. Be prepared to think deeply, to reflect openly and to act steadily as the following pages provide invaluable wisdom and knowledge, applicable to every person on planet Earth."

Fiona Stuart – partner at Ashtons Legal

"Matthew's book is a fascinating warning to those who can't face the idea of death. As a retired solicitor and a vicar, his Book has a practical and a spiritual combination which is informative and soothing at the same time. I enjoyed it very much."

Rupert Everett – actor

"The only certainty in life is death. As a nation we prepare for many things, but rarely for death. Having worked in the funeral industry for over a decade, I have seen the devastation caused to families not only by grief, but also by the uncertainty of their loved one's funeral wishes. Sorting out one's affairs and ensuring this is documented, as Matthew's Book proposes, is an act of love for those who are left behind and will enable them to grieve with the knowledge that they are fulfilling your wishes. Doing this won't hasten your demise, but it will leave clarity."

Lucy Coote - Community Ambassador, Rosedale Funeral Home

CONTENTS

PREFACE

"Enjoy yourself; it's later than you think."
(Horace, Roman lyric poet, BC 65-8)

In October 2019, my wife Annie and I were spending a long weekend with friends, two of whom had been widowed fairly recently. One commented that, apart from the devastating grief of sudden bereavement, she had found herself wishing that her husband had left clear information and instructions on management of the family home and financial affairs. The other (who had had time with her husband to get a reasonable feel of what she needed to know) suggested that leaving as full a record as possible of such things might fairly be regarded as a gift to those left behind: hence, the title of this Book. A number of the married couples present, and others since, also thought that some essentially practical guidance would be very helpful.

The circumstances in which our friends found themselves are not a matter of gender, age, property values or intelligence. Regardless of 'who goes first', far too many couples and indeed individuals have as yet not 'put their affairs in order'.

That got me thinking. As a former private client solicitor, tax adviser, author and lecturer and, more recently, as a vicar in the Church of England, I have long found myself giving pastoral support to people facing death and to their relatives after death. In particular, my previous professional role included putting together a pro forma list of assets and liabilities for completion by the client to help me advise them. How could I develop this idea?

1

"SURPRISE!"

It occurred to me that, if someone thought about the subject at all, they might well just think: –
(a) I must make a Will.
(b) I must outline the funeral arrangements and perhaps pay in advance.

As to (a), over 50% of all UK adults haven't made a Will (and will doubtless be astonished to see the impact of the 'Intestacy Rules' (set out on pages 24-25) which lay down how property is distributed when you die intestate, which means dying without having made a Will.

As for (b), people often haven't given much attention to their funeral arrangements, until perhaps death is looking fairly certain. Moreover, in my experience as an ordained minister, when putting the funeral together, one of the main questions the family ask is, 'What would they have wanted?'

Of course, the subject is so much broader than that. None of us likes to think about our death, but, as Benjamin Franklin famously said, death is one of the *"two certainties in life"* (the other being taxes). So, if, when alive, we spend serious time and energy thinking about our friends and families, work, possessions, holidays and the like, it surely makes sense to give careful thought as to what happens to those we leave behind. Our death affects the overall pattern of our lives.

This Book tries to keep the subject within reasonable bounds. And it's intended to encourage not morbidity, but rather realism. I hope that *My Last Gift* can be seen as part of living life to the full.

> – *"How would you like to die?"*
> – *"At the end of a sentence."*
> (Sir Peter Ustinov, English actor, interviewer,
> film-maker and writer, 1921-2004)

The Format of the Book

There are six Chapters drawing individual topics together under a number of overall headings.

Chapter 1: Your Preparation – For the Inevitable
None of us knows when the 'grim reaper' will strike. In this Chapter I talk about the issues which need to be addressed at whatever stage of your life – starting with 'The Essentials', a list of important questions to answer. I look at Lasting Powers of Attorney in regard to property, financial affairs, health, welfare and the Court of Protection. The Chapter finishes with important matters including guardianship, digital assets and any advance planning of your funeral.

Chapter 2: Some Practicalities – Your Will and any letters of wishes
This Chapter focuses on making a Will and what sort of things it might contain. It will enable you to be sure that those who you want to inherit the various things in your estate do indeed do so.

Chapter 3: The People – Who Matter to You
How can you make sure you spend time with your closest family and friends, and maybe make gifts to them? Then follows the putting together of a list of contact details of people or organisations to be notified after your death.

Chapter 4. Your Possessions – And How to Access them
This Chapter will help your Executors to know what they have to deal with. You need to make some sort of record of what you own (see Appendix 5 on pages 91-93). Succeeding sections of this Chapter deal with a variety of particular assets, for example: your house or flat; bank accounts and investments; insurance(s); cars; photographs; plus papers, letters and files; and your business, if relevant.

Chapter 5: Your Plans for the Future – Thinking them Through
The Chapter starts with a brief description of how Inheritance Tax (traditionally known as 'Death Duties') operates, with some suggestions for reducing the tax bill by way of lifetime gifts. Your focus, wants and needs may well change with age. This includes possibly downsizing your home, perhaps visiting certain places and doing things you have always wanted to do. There is the all-important matter of religious faith too, at least to consider.

Chapter 6: Post-Script – What Happens Afterwards
This Chapter looks ahead to what happens after death, so you can make it as easy as possible for your nearest and dearest. It starts with telling family and close friends (see pages 88-89 for Appendix 4). The funeral director also needs to be contacted, and the funeral put together in accordance with your wishes. The Death Certificate has to be obtained and newspaper announcements considered. There's also the issue of accessing the Will and any Letters of Wishes, plus the process of applying for Probate where required. Probate is the official term for reviewing the validity of your Will and dealing with your property. This includes paying any Inheritance Tax due and other debts.

–"To what do you attribute your long life?"
–"To the fact that I haven't died yet."
(Sir Malcolm Sargent, English orchestral conductor, composer and
interviewer, 1895-1967)

Updates

This is a section on the website www.yourlastgiftbook.com where
any significant developments either in the law or in practice after
publication of the Book will be posted. Also, any amendments to
the text and any notable changes to the content of the forms on the
website will be posted there.

The Appendices, as the 'Guts' of the Book

Above all, this is a practical book. Hence the idea of
Checklists and a variety of forms which you can fill in for
those you leave behind (to update from time to time). These
are set out in the Appendices and can be accessed from the
website www.yourlastgiftbook.com as follows:

1.   The Two Checklists
2.   Personal Details
3.   Whereabouts of Important Documents
4.   People to Contact, in Person, by Telephone or by Email
5.   List of Possessions
6.   Things to Know about your Home.

Appendix 7 lists Some Useful Resources.

The first 'Critical Checklist' is for immediate use. The second,
'Comprehensive Checklist', is intended for more leisurely attention.
Do remember the title of the Book, *Your Last Gift*, which is about
helping those you leave behind. I am conscious that the second
Checklist and the content of the further forms in Appendices 2 to
6 might seem rather formidable. Certainly, it would be practically
impossible for anyone to sit down and fill them all in at a single sitting.

So completion is likely to be a gradual thing – and, indeed, there is no requirement to fill everything in. Some headings will simply not be applicable to you. On the other hand, you may find that, to meet your own circumstances, some subjects are missing from the Appendices, in which case you can simply adapt the content as you choose. The Appendices set out at the back of the Book are for illustrative purposes and have been condensed down for reference only. You will find expanded and fully editable digital versions of these pages available on the website, as updated from time to time, which form a much more practical way to create your own records.

How to Make Best Use of the Book

This is a short book and readable enough to be covered without too much difficulty, perhaps even in a single sitting. There's lots of detail I could have added, but I want to make it as concise as possible. Not every section in the Book will apply to everybody. However, an initial read through will give you an idea of what is relevant to you.

Then perhaps look at the two Checklists in Appendix 1 on pages 75-85. You could start to make a note of what action you would like to take, maybe in discussion with your other half, if you have one. If there are two of you, you might like to do it together, each making up your own version of the various lists and forms. The Book is for you to use as best suits you.

The big question, of course, is where and how to store the information safely. Given that your Will is kept by your solicitor, you might like to make a physical copy to be kept with your Will, as well as leaving one in a secure place at home, perhaps in a safe. To guard against the possible hacking of your computer, you could delete the information from your hard drive and pop the file on a memory stick to be kept with the version in your safe for easy updating. The securest method is undoubtedly the Password Manager suggestion in Chapter 1 on page 18. Using such software means that all your up-to-date passwords to all your internet sites would be available to your family after your death. All you need to do is lodge the Master Password and your sign-in email with your solicitor and keep a copy in your safe.

Do remember that *Your Last Gift* is written by an Englishman for the benefit of those who live in the United Kingdom. So, if you live elsewhere, please make any necessary adjustments.

Finally, maybe a bit paradoxically, I should say that I don't think of this as a book primarily about death. Rather, it's intended to be about life. OK, about the end of that life – and none of us knows when that will happen. But my hope is that the process of following the suggestions may encourage each of us to reflect more deeply on what, and much more importantly who, matter to us most.

"I'm not dying of cancer, I'm living with cancer."
(Deborah Hutton, my late sister whose book *What can I do to help?* is referenced in Appendix 7 on pages 96 and 97, 1955-2005)

CHAPTER 1

YOUR PREPARATION
For the Inevitable

*"There will come a time when you believe everything is finished.
That will be the beginning."*
(Louis L'Amour, American author, 1908-1988)

Setting the Scene

An article in my local newspaper, the Eastern Daily Press, on 15 January 2022 said it all (almost). Nick Copeman, a healthy 43-year-old man, *"has decided to pare back his life and declutter, to prepare his affairs for after his death"*. That involved, first, reducing his possessions to just 406 items, each carefully listed in a database under defined categories. This, the article continued *"is a bizarre extension of another craze – Swedish death cleansing, or döstädning"*. Secondly, *"Mr Copeman has launched a new website, dethprep.com, to chronicle his activities and encourage others to follow his example. The site features a three-step guide to preparing for death. It involves not only creating detailed instructions for your funeral and completing a will, but getting all your financial affairs in order, reducing your possessions, itemising what remains, and working out precisely who will get what after your death"*.

While the article concluded by saying that *"[in] 2003, Mr Copeman [now a copywriter] declared a two-berth caravan at Beeston Bump an empire and crowned himself king of it, changing his name by deed poll to King Nicholas I"*, it does make a serious point by quoting Mr Copeman as saying that he is *"a motivator, not an undertaker"*.

In other words, I'm not alone in suggesting that putting and keeping one's affairs in order is both sensible and kind. Indeed, I have just learned from a friend that she and her partner have created a 'Death Drawer', with copies, mostly on Google Drive, of their Wills, details of passwords, contact information for utility providers etc. However, my impression is that most people have not taken any such steps.

Your Stage of Life

I don't know what 'stage of life' you have reached. You may have a reasonable belief that death might be some distance away or maybe something has happened (perhaps a health scare, if not simply getting older) to suggest that death could be closer to hand. Either way, it's well worth thinking about what you would like to do before the end. Whatever our age or health, we need to address these realities now.

"I intend to live forever. So far, so good."
(Steven Wright, American comedian, actor and
film producer, 1955-   )

The Essentials – The 'Critical Checklist'

1. Who should be the first people to be told about your death – and then who else?
2. If you have minor children, who is to take care of them?
3. If you have pets, who is to look after them?
4. Immediate cash: especially if you handle the money or are much richer than your other half, how is the survivor to access money for necessities until the Grant of Probate which will release funds? The easiest thing to do is to create a joint bank account on which either of you can draw now (and the survivor after your death), with enough money in it to last until Probate is granted.
5. Where are the Passwords to your digital devices and the key or code to your safe (if you have one)?
6. Where is your Will? This needs to be located and read at once. It may say something about your preferred funeral arrangements, quite apart from naming your Executors who will take charge of your affairs. If you haven't got one, then make this a first priority, even if it is in very simple terms which you can revise later (see pages 26-33).
7. Confirm the information which your 'nearest and dearest' will need to register your death, which in England, Wales and Northern Ireland has to be done within five days (see pages 69-70).

Lasting Powers of Attorney

Mental incapacity, specifically dementia, is a sad fact of life for many people. Even physical incapacity of some sort can severely hamper your ability to do things as easily as before.

Wherever you find yourself on the spectrum of life, I strongly recommend making a 'Lasting Power of Attorney' (LPA), which comes in two parts:
• Property and Financial Affairs
• Health and Welfare.

Basically, you are appointing one or more people close to you who you completely trust to take over responsibility for making important decisions on your behalf if needed. Failure to do that and loss of mental capacity will typically lead to a much more complex and potentially long-drawn-out process, whereby the individual's affairs are put into the hands of the Court of Protection (and you really don't want to go there).

To make your LPA, and to register it, consult a solicitor (see page 24 in Chapter 2 on Professional Advisers), though it is possible to do it yourself (see the website mentioned in Appendix 7 on page 98).

Once made, the LPA is registered with the Office of the Public Guardian which stamps it with 'VALIDATED – OPG'. Note that the OPG charges a fee of £82 per person per LPA (as at 1 November 2022). The LPA can then simply be filed away (whether at home or with your solicitor) until needed if ever. At that point (and it can be checked with your doctor), your 'attorneys' can take over responsibility for your affairs. They would start by telling your family and friends, your doctor and people looking after you plus any professional advisers. Typically, doctors and any others acting in a professional capacity would want to see proof of your identity and either the original LPA or a certified copy.

You can appoint one individual to act as your attorney or more than one. If more than one, they can be appointed either 'jointly' or 'severally'. 'Jointly' requires that they must make a unanimous decision on acting. If 'severally', then any one of them can act. The LPA could provide that some decisions have to be taken jointly, some severally and others 'jointly and severally' (which means that your attorneys can make decisions together or alternatively act individually if they need to).

Often the loss of mental capacity is gradual rather than sudden. So there may be a time when your attorney(s) are working with you to make your own decisions. In any case, the attorney(s) must follow the terms of the LPA and make all decisions in your best interests. Guidance is available on how to do this.

"Old age isn't so bad when you consider the alternative."
(Maurice Chevalier, French singer and actor, 1888-1972)

Property and Financial Affairs

Decisions here might concern:
- handling bank and building society accounts
- paying bills
- arranging for tax returns to be filed and paid
- starting, continuing or varying payments from pensions
- receiving benefits
- managing investments
- dealing with property.

Health and Welfare

This covers decisions on:
- living arrangements
- medical care
- daily routine.

While you may appoint different people as your Property and Financial Affairs Attorney and your Health and Welfare Attorney, very often they will be the same. If not, any financial decisions touching on your living arrangements, care or lifestyle would be up for discussion with your Health and Welfare Attorney.

Authorise your Health and Welfare Attorney to do their best to ensure that your wishes for medical treatment are honoured. A 'Living Will' is a legal statement from you, which the Attorney would give to the hospital staff along with the LPA. The NHS call it an 'advance decision'. So for example, you might not want to be kept alive by a ventilator (if you cannot breathe by yourself) or by resuscitation (cardiopulmonary resuscitation or CPR) if your heart stops beating or by antibiotics. The advance decision is signed by you in front of a witness. If you wish to refuse such treatment in circumstances where you might die, you should say so.

"WAIT - DO THEY MEAN NO TO THE VENTILATOR OR THE VENTILATION?"

This is a very complex and sensitive area. You may wish to discuss the content of an advance decision with a suitably qualified doctor or nurse and/or someone who knows you well. By contrast, an 'advance statement' is a more informal guide stating how you would like to be looked after if you can no longer communicate properly. An advance statement is not legally binding, as is an advance decision. It doesn't have to be witnessed or even signed (though ideally it is).

The ReSPECT Form

As a less formal alternative to an advance decision, you could consider the ReSPECT Form (Version 3) introduced in 2016 by the Resuscitation Council UK. ReSPECT stands for Recommended Summary Plan for Emergency Care and Treatment process, to formalise conversations between the patient, their family and healthcare professionals about care in a future emergency. The Resuscitation Council UK website (see page 99) says:

"As patients are often not able to make decisions about their priorities of care or treatment in an emergency, discussing what they would want to happen in advance is important. One of the key issues, but not the only one, is whether cardiopulmonary resuscitation (CPR) should be applied in a future emergency."

This two-page fairly streamlined form is divided into nine sections:

1. Summary details
2. Shared understanding of my health and current condition
3. What matters to me in decisions about my treatment and care in an emergency
4. Clinical recommendations for emergency care and treatment
5. Capacity for involvement in making this plan
6. Involvement in making this plan
7. Clinicians' signatures
8. Emergency contacts and those involved in discussing this plan
9. Form reviewed (e.g. for change of care setting) and remains relevant

"The doctor said 'I have good news and bad news. The good news is that you're not a hypochondriac.'"
(Bob Monkhouse, English comedian, writer and actor, 1928-2003)

The Court of Protection

Once an individual has lost mental capacity, he/she can no longer make an LPA. So an application has to be made to the Court of Protection for someone to become a 'deputy' in order to make decisions on their behalf. The application can be complex, time-consuming and expensive, and until the appointment is made, no financial or welfare decisions can be taken.

Guardians for Minor Children

While you and your spouse/partner are young and have minor children, think carefully as to who you would like to look after them if you both die when any of them are under the age of 18. It may be a relative or close friend, with whom you should discuss financial provision, values, special needs of a particular child and how they will fit in with the guardian's own family.

This would be a decision to be kept under review. It is one best made by Will, appointing 'Testamentary Guardians' (see page 74).

Pets

Any pets will doubtless take your death hard too. If you leave a surviving spouse, partner or someone else you live with, maybe they can carry on looking after them, at least in the short term. If not, nominate an agreed person to take on the animals. Any insurance policies relating to your pets you will need to list and leave clear instructions for the nominated person(s). See page 76 for the Critical Checklist.

"I'm not afraid to die, I just don't want to be there when it happens."
(Woody Allen, American film director, actor and comedian, 1935-   )

Digital Assets

This is potentially quite a challenge – even a legal minefield. These include:

- computer
- tablet/iPad
- mobile telephone
- social media
- Dropbox and other facilities.

How will you provide continuing access to your email account(s), which will give your Executors a good idea of which online services you have been using and, where passwords might be unknown or lost, could be the means of accessing other accounts by way of a password reset? In the event of your death, what security information will be needed to continue access? In particular, you need to ensure that your death does not have the effect of cancelling access to any of your digital devices or electronic accounts. See below for the Computer Misuse Act 1990.

In addition to these passwords, you will typically use a range of passwords for a whole variety of associations and memberships. There will also be rights to property such as an online bank account, online share portfolio or PayPal account. Then there may be digital records of photographs, videos, documents, letters and so on. What matters is that whoever you appoint has the ability to do so lawfully through the service provider. Your Executors will have the right to access your various electronic devices through your passwords, whereas for Cloud Accounts they will need the Account ID.

So, at the very least, include in your checklist a note on the whereabouts of the passwords required to access your computer and other electronic devices. The best solution is to use a 'Password Manager' to keep all your passwords safely and keep the single 'master password' in an utterly secure place. By contrast, if the master password is kept somewhere deep within your own device, a potential hacker would need both the knowledge of the existence of the master password and control of the device itself, to gain access. A whole range of Password Managers is available, which you can find from Google.

Even if you do not go for the Password Manager solution, you should, if you do nothing else, leave a list of passwords to all your devices in a safe place and tell one or more people who are almost certain to survive you where that place is. Ensuring that your next of kin has/ have access to passwords is essential for alleviating stress after you go.

Not all Digital Assets constitute property rights, so forming part of your Estate to be administered by your Executor(s) in the ordinary way. Hence, the Will should give your Executor(s) an express power to deal with such 'non-property Digital Assets'. Alternatively, you could appoint a Digital Manager to do the job. You should direct your Estate to repay any costs falling on either the Executors or the Digital Manager. This underlies the importance of an up-to-date list of all your assets, including Digital Assets.

Any important records such as a collection of photographs would ideally be stored in the Cloud, for example on Apple's iCloud or Google Photos. However, it could be difficult to access this after your death, so have a back-up of such records on your own device.

As with all Cloud Accounts, give careful thought to who has the authority to deal with the particular account. Bear in mind that a simple list of passwords may not be the answer, as logging in using someone else's details could be a criminal offence[1] (unless the account is owned by a business and this is allowed). If this sounds scary, distinguish between your Executors using your passwords to gain access to your devices, which is completely permissible, and your Executors using your passwords to log on to online accounts, which is potentially problematic.

Check with the account provider as to what happens when you die and how you provide access to the chosen person. For example, Facebook allow you to appoint a Legacy Contact.

All this should be kept outside the terms of your Will, since once probate is granted, they will be open for anyone to view.

Cryptocurrency

Cryptocurrency is a different matter. Here there is no other person from whom your Executors can get access to the asset. It is essential to take specific advice to ensure that what might be quite a substantial value is not lost. Appendix 7 (Some Useful Resources) notes a recommended short and practical book on page 97.

"My grandmother was a very tough woman. She buried three husbands and two of them were just napping."
(Rita Rudner, American comedian, 1953-)

Burial or Cremation?

You may want to leave details of your preferred funeral directors. Perhaps you will have appointed them beforehand. Funeral costs are traditionally horrendously expensive and many people take out a funeral plan in

---

[1] Under the Computer Misuse Act 1990 section 1.

advance. My late mother embraced life with both generosity and passion – while at the same time she was a force to be reckoned with and indeed a bit of a wheeler dealer. Her untrammelled enthusiasm for new ideas led to her involvement in quite a number of business enterprises. These included an eco-cardboard coffin start-up business where you could have an illustration of your choice on your coffin and keep it under your bed to be whipped out when needed! We were surprised (and, indeed, rather relieved) when she did eventually die to find that she had forgotten to arrange one for herself.

Whether or not you go for a religious service/ceremony/memorial, in my experience the family do value the fact that the arrangements have been made in advance. This is not just because it is one less thing 'to do', but also they then know that they are acting in accordance with your wishes. It may be convenient to leave a Letter of Wishes with your Will. You would make it clear whether you would like a Christian or other faith ceremony and whether you would prefer to be cremated or buried. If the latter, especially in a churchyard, it is helpful for arrangements to be made in advance. While what follows takes the form of a Christian service, it can equally be adapted if you are of another faith or none.

"I want to wake up dead"
(Bridget Leppard, my late mother-in-law, 1925-2016)

The most straightforward course is a funeral service at a church followed by a burial in the churchyard – and then a 'wake' or party, whether in your home or village hall or indeed elsewhere. If you prefer to be cremated, do check on the length of service permitted at the particular crematorium. It could be just 30 minutes at the outside, although it is possible to book (and pay for) two slots to give one longer. A cremation can be followed by a church service – or the service could come first, depending on logistics. It is probably most convenient for both to happen on the same day, perhaps limiting the cremation to close family members and friends, with a larger attendance in church. Then there would be the wake, the cost of which is happily deductible for Inheritance Tax purposes.

It is always possible to have a memorial service some months later. Even if you aren't a person of local or even national significance, a large number of people might wish to celebrate your life.

As to the service, particular things you could include in a Letter of Wishes are:
- who takes the service
- choice of hymns and other music
- Bible (or other sacred text) readings
- other readings
- who else you would like to present readings etc at the service
- who gives the tribute(s)
- who gives a homily on the Bible (or sacred text) passage chosen
- music both coming and going out and perhaps during the service.

Forms/Lists

The Appendices include seven flexible documents which purchase of this Book will enable you to access from the website www.yourlastgiftbook.com for you to adapt to your own circumstances, fill in yourself and amend from time to time as necessary. The forms on the website are subject to updating, so they may not be exactly the same as the versions in this Book.

These are:
1. Checklists, Critical and Comprehensive
2. Personal Details
3. Whereabouts of Important Documents
4. People to Contact
5. List of Possessions
6. Things to Know about your Home.

See the Preface on page 6 for the secure storage of these documents.

CHAPTER 2

SOME PRACTICALITIES
On Your Will and any Letters of Wishes

"Death is more universal than life; everyone dies
but not everyone lives."
(Andrew Sachs, English actor, 1930-2016)

Setting the Scene

There was a man who had a very valuable art collection. On his death his Executors are instructed to hold an auction of his collection. The impressive collection drums up interest from far and wide and many people attend the auction. The first lot, an unsigned picture of a boy, has no value. No-one bids on it until there is a murmur from the back of the room. The deceased man's old housekeeper bids her small amount of savings for it and the hammer comes down. The auctioneer then stops the auction, saying that the remaining lots will now go to the housekeeper, as the deceased specified that "the person who buys the painting of my son gets it all." True or not, the story emphasises that you can do what you want with your Will (more or less) and that, to achieve your wishes, you can be quite creative.

Professional Advisers

Whether or not you have regular professional advisers, perhaps accountants involved in your tax return or solicitors previously instructed in relation to a property purchase or your Will, make sure that those who are looking after your affairs post-death do have the contact details. These could include land agents or estate agents in terms of valuing property, insurers who might be able to recommend a valuer for personal possessions, jewellery and so on. A particular word about solicitors. A Will should in my view be reviewed every five years – or sooner in the event of a significant change in circumstances. Choosing a solicitor is important, not just in drawing up your Will, but also as someone with whom the survivors will get on really well with and trust after your death. If you don't have such a solicitor, ask local friends for a good recommendation.

What Happens if You Don't Make a Will – The Intestacy Rules (as at 1 November 2022)

What follows can be quite sobering and not what many people expect. These are the rules for England and Wales, while Scotland and Northern Ireland are different.

If a person dies leaving a spouse/civil partner but no children, the whole estate is paid to the spouse/civil partner. However, if there are children surviving, then:

- the surviving spouse/civil partner will receive a 'statutory legacy' of £270,000 plus all personal possessions,
- the surviving spouse/civil partner is also entitled absolutely to half the residuary estate (which means, 'what is left'), and
- the other half is divided equally between the surviving children, who become entitled absolutely at age 18.

If there is no surviving spouse or civil partner, then there is a set of rules which dictates who inherits. First, children in equal shares – but if a child has already died, then his or her children step into that parent's shoes, in equal shares if more than one. If no children, then surviving parents inherit equally. Then brothers and sisters and so on. In the absence of any surviving blood relatives, the whole estate goes to the Crown.

The vital point is that if you live with someone who is neither your spouse or civil partner, then however long and stable the relationship, there is no legal entitlement for the survivor – in the absence of a Will. This includes a share in the home owned by the person who has died. A lot of people don't realise this, imagining that a so-called 'common law wife/husband' has the same rights as if they were married. The same point arises with the exemption from Inheritance Tax (see page 60).

"If you die in an elevator, be sure to push the UP button."
(Sam Levenson, American comedian, writer, television host and journalist, 1911-1980)

Making and Updating Your Will –
and any Letters of Wishes

While you can make a homemade Will, I strongly advise that you 'instruct' a solicitor. That way lies certainty. The expense should be relatively modest, unless some tax planning is required at the same time. This will ensure that those you want to inherit your property will do so – and that your wishes will be honoured. Alternatively, there is a variety of websites from which you can create a simple Will for a fraction of the cost.

There is a story about my ancestor Daisy Singer Alexander, granddaughter of the sewing machine inventor Isaac Singer. Daisy hadn't quite got her affairs in order. She did make a Will, which she signed and put in a bottle which she sent off to sea. The Will left her Estate (then worth US $12 million) to the person who found the bottle with the Will inside. On 16 March 1949 (12 years after Daisy's death), one Jack J. Wurm from Palo Alto was walking along a beach near San Francisco when he noticed a bottle washed up on the sand. The note in the bottle read "To avoid all confusion I leave my entire estate to the lucky person who finds this bottle and to my attorney, Barry Cohen, share and share alike. Daisy Alexander – June 20, 1937". There was no other record of the Will which might have proved its authenticity. In fact, Jack Wurm did not receive a penny, after the Singer family contested the Will. The official website of the Singer sewing machine company dismisses the story as an 'urban legend'. The moral? Make sure you engage a solicitor to draw up your Will, to ensure that it's properly signed, witnessed and kept safe.

A Will has to be witnessed by two disinterested individuals (so remember that, if you witness a Will, you can't benefit from it – if a close relative happens to invite you to witness the signing of their Will!). Remember, too, that all the witnesses are witnessing is your signature and not the content of the document – just in case they get nosy …

Will Procedure

The Will normally proceeds as follows:

1. You state your full name and address, revoking all former Wills and stating that it is the Law of England and Wales which applies[2].

2. You say whether you wish your body to be buried or cremated. Whichever you choose, specify where in the case of a burial and with a cremation where you might like your ashes to be scattered. Equally, the place can be specified in a Letter of Wishes (which is easier to change).

3. You appoint one or more individuals as your Executor(s), giving their name and address. Ask first if they are prepared to undertake the task. Sometimes acting as an Executor can be time-consuming and, depending on your relationship with them, it is quite nice to leave them a cash gift or 'legacy'. Ideally, there should be two Executors, though perhaps only one if it is to be a surviving spouse or partner. Executors have to act unanimously and, in appointing them, you need to ensure not only that you trust them, but that you can rely on them to act dispassionately and honourably in the interests of the Beneficiaries as a whole, especially if one or more of your Executors also happens to be a Beneficiary. I have just heard a sad and salutary account of where this didn't happen, with big fall-out in both property values and relationships.

"Let's choose executors and talk of wills;
And yet not so – for what can we bequeath
Save our deposed bodies to the ground?"
(William Shakespeare, King Richard II, Act 3, Scene 2,
English playwright, 1564-1616)

---

[2] Unless you wish to apply the law of Scotland or of Northern Ireland.

The appointment of an Executor will typically be subject to the condition that he or she survives you by 30 days. You might then, failing that, appoint replacement Executors. Bear in mind that if an Executor dies before the Estate has been administered, the 'chain of executorship' applies, under which the Executors of that deceased Executor step into his or her shoes. This can seem a bit strange. Once the death has occurred, it is not possible for different Executors to be appointed (except under the chain of executorship).

Choosing your Executors is a serious business. A spouse/partner and/or one or more children might be your first choice. You don't want them to die before you, so you might appoint slightly younger people. You can specify in your Will who should take the place of any Executor who dies before you. They should be people you trust and who know the family. I always advise against choosing a firm of solicitors or a bank as Executors.

4. The Will usually refers to the Executor 'as Executor and Trustee', which can seem a bit confusing. Normally once the Estate has been 'administered', that is, all the assets 'gathered in', all debts paid, including to His Majesty's Revenue and Customs or HMRC (previously the Inland Revenue), and the assets distributed according to the Will, the role of the Executors will come to an end and they will 'sign off' the final estate accounts (typically prepared by the solicitors).

However, the Will might have created continuing trusts. This means that there is property which is not left outright and has to be administered. In this case, while the Executors' roles come to an end, they or others may be appointed as Trustees to continue to look after the property. There would certainly be a trust if the beneficiaries were under 18. Or it may be that you are concerned about giving significant assets to those, even if aged 18 or over, who you feel do not have the maturity or knowledge to deal with them properly. If so, you might create a formal trust. A trust separates the ownership of capital from an entitlement to income. While the capital remains in the hands of the Trustees, the income will typically be paid out each year to the beneficiaries who will get to enjoy the capital in due course (if not accumulated for a permitted period). All of this would be set out in the Will and discussed with you by your solicitor.

5. If you have young children, you will want to appoint 'Testamentary Guardians' (see page 74).

6. There could be cash gifts or legacies to named individuals or charities.

"When you've told someone that you've left them a legacy, the only decent thing to do is to die at once."
(Samuel Butler, English novelist and critic, 1835-1902)

7. 'Bequests' are gifts of certain types of property – perhaps jewellery, pictures, a collection you have built up over your lifetime or even a house or flat. You will usually want to state that any gift of cash or other property will be free of tax; the burden of any Inheritance Tax will fall on 'what is left' in the Estate - the 'residue'. As a practical suggestion, if you have any children or indeed grandchildren, you might like to mention each of them as the recipient of one or more things which you have specifically chosen for them. The fact that you have taken the trouble to select something will mean a lot.

8. Then there is the gift of residue made to your Executors to pay any tax or other debts due and to hold on trust to distribute to one or more individuals, perhaps in prescribed proportions.

9. There will follow a range of powers given to your Executors to deal with your property, much as if they owned it themselves. Traditionally, these powers were set out in full in the Will. Now it is common to short circuit the process by referring to the current edition of a commonly accepted list of powers set up by the Society of Trust and Estate Practitioners (STEP)[3].

[3] www.step.org

10. Sometimes you might write, and from time to time update, one or more 'Letters of Wishes'. These cover any discretions you have given to your Executors. For example, you may not wish your children to inherit property before the age of 30, but you want to give your Executors power to make a gift of all or a given percentage before that age, in which case you could set out in the Letter of Wishes the sort of things you wish the Executors to consider before making that decision. A Letter of Wishes is much more informal than a Will, both in not having to be witnessed and in being easier to change. Further, it is not a 'public document' (a Will is available for all to see once probate has been granted: see page 73). That said, for the sake of certainty, any Letters of Wishes should be kept with the Will, ideally with your Solicitor.

"Don't send me flowers when I'm dead. If you like me, send them while I'm alive."
(Brian Clough, English football player and manager, 1935-2004)

Achieving 'Fairness'

The general 'freedom of testamentary disposition' in the UK means that you can leave in your Will what you like to whom you like[4]. For example, a share in a family business or a farm which is left to one particular child rather than to all the children equally, in the hope that this will help the asset to survive within the family to pass down to future generations.

That case apart, you may want your children to receive the same or similar values of 'liquid assets', specifically cash or stocks and shares. The important thing is that your children – and any other relevant members of the family – understand that you have tried to be fair and that you love them all equally (assuming that to be the case!) – and so, in the case of the family business or farm just mentioned, you may choose to explain to the children why you have taken this course.

---

[4] However, note that special 'legal rights' rules apply in Scotland. And note also the qualification presented by the Inheritance (Provision for Family and Other Dependents) Act 1975 discussed on page 32, under which a member of the family or a dependent can, in certain circumstances, challenge a provision in the Will which leaves them nothing or very little.

Suppose you have three children: Anne, Bertie and Caroline. In 2018, you gave £5,000 to Anne. In 2019, you lent £10,000 interest-free to Bertie on vague repayment terms. You have never given or lent a significant sum to Caroline. You have treated all of them more or less equally in terms of Birthday and Christmas presents. Other than, say, giving £5,000 to Anne, writing off the loan to Bertie (which should be done formally by what is called a Deed, where the signatures are witnessed and would take effect as a gift of £10,000 to Bertie made now) and giving £10,000 to Caroline, how might you correct the position under your Will if you choose to do so? The sums in this example are fairly simple. It may well be that over the years you have made a whole range of gifts and maybe loans to your children.

The first step is to make a list which you would keep up to date – and leave with your Will. Either you could create equality now in the way suggested in the previous paragraph, if depending on the figures you can afford it (which should be more Inheritance Tax efficient), or you could ask your solicitors to put into your Will a 'Discretionary Legacy', either through a new Will or by a Codicil (which is a simple document adding to or amending your Will, without going to the trouble of making a whole new Will).

The clause would give to your Executors the sum of £x free of Inheritance Tax for them to distribute equally among your children [or indeed any other beneficiaries, e.g. nephews and nieces], so that taking account of the list of gifts and loans made to them during your lifetime, each would end up with more or less the same amount. The sum of £x would be calculated by reference to both the total and the individual amounts in your list, as the minimum needed to achieve equality: in my example, this would be £15,000, with £5,000 given to Anne, £10,000 given to Caroline and the loan to Bertie written off (which would take effect as a gift of £10,000 to him under the Will). If you wanted to use this mechanism to even up any imbalance in the values of chattels taken under your Will, on the basis of professional valuations, you could increase £x accordingly.

Post-death events

The 'freedom of testamentary disposition' mentioned on page 30 above is subject to one very important proviso, which is worth bearing in mind. The Inheritance (Provision for Family and Dependents) Act 1975 allows a surviving cohabiting partner and anyone treated as family or being maintained by the deceased to claim on the estate. So if there is anyone within that description who is left very little or nothing under the Will, they may be able to challenge it in Court under the 1975 Act. While its application needs very specific advice, the existence of the Act may deter someone from making a Will who wants to cut somebody out altogether, in order to forestall the possibility of a claim, which can be both messy and expensive.

One way of trying to defeat a 1975 Act claim in advance could be through a pre- or post-marital agreement, for example in preparation for a second marriage where a couple want to see that the interests of the children of earlier marriages are protected in the event of dissolution of a second marriage. That said, such agreements may not be enforceable in the court as contracts and require specialist legal advice.

While we do in this country generally have testamentary freedom (see note 4 on page 30), you should bear in mind that a Will can generally always be 'varied' within two years of your death. The original beneficiary can make a document to redirect the property to someone else. Provided that the statutory provisions[5] are followed, the substituted gift is written back into the Will. This avoids the on-gift having any Inheritance Tax implications in its own right. For example, an original donee child could redirect property to their own children ('generation skipping'), so that if that donee were to die within seven years of the on-gift, that would carry no Inheritance Tax implications. Further, the rule does not apply for Income Tax purposes.[6]

[5] Under the Inheritance Tax Act 1984 section 142.

[6] So, if Alice were left £1,000 by her aunt, she could by a Deed of Variation made within two years of her aunt's death redirect the gift to charity, with the Inheritance Tax exemption for gifts to charity carried back into her aunt's estate, and with Gift Aid relief from Income Tax given to Alice (and the charity), provided that Alice is a taxpayer who pays a sufficient amount of tax in the tax year – and especially beneficial to her if she is a higher rate taxpayer.

A similar principle applies with gifts under a Will to a discretionary trust[7]: the content of a formal Deed of Gift by the Trustees to a beneficiary within two years after the death is written back into the Will. However, the use of this rule brings only Inheritance Tax and not also Income Tax advantages. Bear in mind that, as mentioned, the Will is a public document. So if you would prefer to keep the details of 'who gets what' outside the public domain, you could use the idea under section 144 of leaving property on discretionary trusts and relying on your Trustees to make an appointment within two years after your death in accordance with a Letter of Wishes (which no-one else will see).

"How people die remains in the memory of those who live on"
(Dame Cicely Saunders, English nurse, social worker and
hospice movement pioneer, 1918-2005)

Foreign Property

A staggering 500,000 or so UK citizens own a second home abroad, the vast majority within Europe. For illustration, take Jack and Jill who live in Leeds and own a holiday home in the South of France. They should take advice from both their British and French lawyers. It is likely that they will be advised to make separate Wills under French law to deal with the French property and under UK law to deal with assets in the UK and indeed elsewhere in the world outside France (unless of course land is concerned, when a further Will under the relevant jurisdiction would be advisable). Jack and Jill might be quite surprised to hear that (unlike the UK) many other countries have quite restricted regimes (called 'community of property' regimes) under which particular percentages of the property have to be left to prescribed classes of beneficiary.

---

[7] Under the Inheritance Tax Act 1984 section 144.

Organ Donation

You may want one or more of your organs (if in good working order) to be used to help, or even save the life of, someone else after you die. Look at the NHS website[8] for more detail. In short, what used to be an 'opt in' system has become an 'opt out'. So if you don't wish your organs to be donated, record your decision on the NHS Organ Donor Register and amend it at any time (see page 98).

[8] www.organdonation.nhs.uk

Be Aware of 'The Procedure' Post-Death

The more arrangements for your nearest and dearest you can make in advance, the better (generally, see Chapter 6 on pages 67-74). The whole process can be distressing, even if necessary, and so whatever you can do to 'sweeten the pill', it will be seen as a gift. This might include:

- Notifications: close family or friends to ring (or even tell in person) and others (at greater leisure) to email
- Newspaper announcements
- Obtaining the Death Certificate
- Accessing and becoming aware of the content of the Will and any Letter(s) of Wishes
- Whether you would like to be buried or cremated, including contact details of your preferred funeral directors
- Putting together your preferred religious service/ceremony/memorial
- If purchased, the whereabouts of your pre-paid funeral plan, making sure that the provider of the plan is authorised by the Financial Conduct Authority
- The Probate Procedure
- 'Moving Forward'.

"Life can only be understood backwards,
but it must be lived forwards."
(Søren Kierkegaard, Danish theologian, philosopher and
religious author, 1813 – 1855)

CHAPTER 3

THE PEOPLE
Who Matter to You

*"My most treasured possessions are not things, they are only
things, my friends, family and animals are what counts."*
(Dame Olivia Newton-John AC, British-Australian actress
and singer, 1948-2022)

Setting the Scene

I want to highlight the very wise and compassionate foresight of my dear sister Debbie, who died far too young at the age of 49 in 2005, and her husband Charlie. Having been diagnosed with Stage four cancer (from which she died peacefully eight months later) and with four children Archie, Romilly, Clemmie and Freddie (then aged between 17 and 8), they took the brave and, in those circumstances, correct decision both to tell the children and to take them with them on the journey.

I acknowledge that such openness won't be the right thing to do in every case. Here, the judgment was proved right by the extraordinarily rich relationships both within and outside the family which already existed and which continued up to and since her death. But, at least, it is a subject which parents should discuss freely with each other, faced with the possible loss of one of them. There is, of course, the issue of appointing testamentary guardians, to look after any children once both parents have died (see page 74).

I deal intentionally in this Book with People ahead of Possessions (or 'Stuff'). I think this is true both of relationships in life and of memories after your death. While I may well be stating 'the bleedin' obvious', I want to encourage each of us (myself included) to think very intentionally about who it is that matter most to us (and maybe we to them) – and why.

"Grief is the price we pay for love."
(HM Queen Elizabeth II, first in 2001 in memory of the 9/11 bombing victims and then on 18 April 2021, reflecting on the death of Prince Philip, 1926-2022)

Family and Good Friends

So much of life simply 'happens', given the sheer pace of life or job/
volunteering or pastimes with which we get caught up. A good thing
about long-standing (rather than 'old') friends is that it's always easy
to pick up where you left off. But once you start reflecting on death,
you may want to think about whom you want to see again, particularly
if it has been a while, and with whom you want to spend time. This
may involve rekindling old friendships, always bearing in mind that
'it takes two to tango'.

Part of that 'spending time with' may involve making clear how
much that person means to you. One suggestion is to write letters to
favourite family members or friends, letters which could be left with
your Will or in a safe place with instructions to deliver them once you
have gone. It is worth keeping copies of all such letters and the dates,
in case you want to rewrite them.

"LOOK WHO COMES CRAWLING BACK..."

Think about making gifts to favourite people. Such gifts could be non-monetary, for example a photograph of a happy holiday or time spent together. Or you might want to give them a book, or something a bit more valuable, such as a painting, some silver or anything else which would mean a lot to them. Such gifts can be left by Will (see page 29) or indeed given while you are still alive, for example tax-efficiently making use of the available lifetime exemptions from Inheritance Tax (see pages 60-62), maybe within the £3,000 annual exemption.

Each of us has a variety of relationships. Especially as you get older, you can be intentional about time spent with family and friends, with providing for family (insofar as you can) definitely a priority. Sometimes things happen in life which cause a rift. So, where you are conscious of 'unfinished business' with anyone, you may want to do your best to put it right, whether it's a matter of forgiving them or, if you are 'the guilty party', asking for forgiveness. That way, you can, indeed, 'rest in peace'.

"The bitterest tears shed over a grave are for words left unsaid or deeds left undone."
(Harriet Beecher Stowe, American author and slavery abolitionist 1811-1896)

Contact List for Use Post-Death

Set out in Appendix 4 (pages 88-89), this ties in with the second section of Chapter 6 (pages 68-69). There will be those closest to you whom you would want to be notified by telephone and certainly not by email. Perhaps this is a job to be parcelled out between family members. Then there may be people who can be emailed, perhaps after some days have passed, if they don't see a newspaper announcement.

Your bank will need to be told and supplied with an official Death Certificate. The account will effectively get frozen (apart from paying a few specified expenses, such as funeral directors) until probate is obtained by your Executors (see pages 49 and 73).

Then there are professional advisers such as accountants, solicitors, insurance brokers, estate agents and the like. For each, you should provide contact details, again to receive one or more official Death Certificates.

The original Death Certificate is held by the Government's General Register Office, which will, on request, issue official copies for a fee, though they look like originals, as bearing an official raised stamp. Many financial institutions require 'original' copies[9] issued by the Registrar of Deaths etc in order to record and act on a death. With an estate of any substance, it is often worth asking for 10 or more 'office copy' certificates when the death is registered.

Finally, there may be a range of clubs, associations or other organisations to which you belong or have had dealings with who will need to be notified. An email, with a simple photocopied Death Certificate attached, would be fine.

[9] Also called 'office copies'.

CHAPTER 4

YOUR POSSESSIONS
And How to Access Them

"There are far, far better things ahead than any we leave behind"
(C.S. Lewis, English author, academic and lay theologian, 1898-1963)

Setting the Scene

This is a true story from my family which illustrates how tax planning can work in conjunction with advance asset planning to produce harmonious distribution of family property after a death. The broad Inheritance Tax rule for lifetime giving is that a gift to one or more individuals made at least seven years before death has no Inheritance Tax implications, so long as the donor enjoys (or 'reserves') no benefit from the gift (see page 60). If full market value (in terms of an annual 'rent') is paid for the enjoyment, there's no benefit reserved.

In 1998, my late mother called a family meeting for my three sisters and me. She had divided all her personal possessions into various lists according to category, e.g. furniture, ornaments, lamps, pictures, jewellery and so on. We four 'children' drew lots to decide who would start, first by selecting a category and then to determine the order of choice, both of which moved round the table. The process continued, with not a little fun and games. A careful list was made of the selection, with approximate values added and, in the end, equality of overall values was obtained through a clause in the Will.

Professional valuers were instructed to put a market value on each item (in fact, two firms of valuers, one acting for the donor, the other for the donee) and also to agree the appropriate annual 'rent'. Our solicitors drew up four Deeds of Gift, including provision for the annual payment of rent, which were duly signed. Mum continued to enjoy the property until the day she died, in 2010 (at least seven years after the gift). Mum paid each of us an annual rent, on which we paid Income Tax. Everyone was happy – even HMRC, as while they may have missed out on the extra Inheritance Tax, they did get some additional Income Tax each year.

Make a List

Once somebody dies, the responsibility for dealing with what they owned – and paying off any debts – falls to the Executors (or, if no Will appointing them, Administrators). While everyone should understand the importance of choosing the right Executors, that doesn't always happen (see also pages 24-25).

It will help your Executors enormously if they have an up-to-date detailed list from which they can work. Typically, this will be things that have monetary value, which you could estimate, though the Executors will have to provide market valuations at the date of death when applying for Probate[10].

This exercise might focus your mind on whether you want to leave specific things to particular people, considered on page 29. I have provided a pro forma list in Appendix 5 (on pages 91-93), for you to adapt for your own purposes.

Think about Who should Get What – and When

Once you have made a list of what you own, think about who you might like to receive particular things. This is likely to happen following your death. However, one of the advantages of making a lifetime gift is that you get the pleasure of receiving a thank you letter and, if the value is significant, there may also be tax advantages (see pages 60-61). If the lifetime gift is of significant value, then the date and a description of the gift and its value should be recorded and left with your papers, since this may affect the Inheritance Tax ultimately payable. Also, bear in mind that monetary value is not everything. A child or other relative may place a lot of value on something which has no or very little monetary value.

"Buying presents for old people is a problem. I would rather like it if people came to my house and took things away."
(Sir Clement Freud, English broadcaster and MP, 1924-2009)

Your House/Flat and any Other Land

You may own or you may rent your home – and, indeed, any other residences, whether in the UK or abroad. The ownership or lease may

---

[10] Probate is the authority of the Court for those individuals to act in relation to what is called your 'Estate', that is, what you own. See Chapter 6 page 73.

be in your sole name or held jointly with someone else, for example your spouse or partner. Under English law, there are two types of joint ownership:

• A 'joint tenancy' (even if the property is freehold) under which each joint tenant has an equal share. On the death of any joint tenant, his/her share passes automatically 'by operation of law' to the surviving joint tenant(s) and if more than one in equal shares. This is a common arrangement with a married couple and the principle applies to other types of property, e.g. bank accounts (see pages 11 and 49). If the survivor is a spouse/civil partner, remember that the exemption from Inheritance Tax will apply, but that in any other case there may be Inheritance Tax implications; similarly, with a tenancy in common, below.

• A 'tenancy in common' (again, which can apply to a freehold) under which the share of any so-called 'tenant in common' is an asset owned that can be specifically given by Will – or indeed by lifetime gift. Shares under a tenancy in common can be unequal.

In either case, the value of the interest in the property is an asset of the deceased, the value of which must be ascertained and included for probate purposes. That said, unless the other joint owner is a surviving spouse or civil partner, there will typically be a valuation discount of 10% for Inheritance Tax purposes.

In any event, your possessions will need to be removed from the property. Think about who would do this: it can be onerous task, though sweetened if those with the responsibility will also inherit.

If you rent your home, especially if you are the only tenant, obviously the landlord should be notified and the terms of the lease consulted, in case there is a continuing liability to pay rent (and other services) for a particular period of time. It may be possible to bring the lease to an end early.

Even if a flat or house is subject to a long lease, for which you have paid a lump sum premium (where there may also be a continuing liability for annual ground rents), the freeholder (which may be a company) will have to be notified, as well as perhaps a residents' association or management company. Again, the value of the remaining lease will be an asset in your estate. As also where the house or flat is owned freehold. Where the flat is freehold, typically you will have a long lease, with the freehold owned by a company in which you own one or more shares.

Either a lease or a freehold may be subject to a mortgage. The mortgage company (or 'mortgagee') should be notified. Death will end the automatic debit of monthly repayments and so your Executors will need to agree with the bank or building society the placing on hold of these until probate is granted or whether other arrangements can be made for payment meanwhile.

Details of all the above are listed in Appendix 4 (People to Contact on pages 88-89) for you to complete, as well as details of utilities etc, all of which will need to be notified (see Appendix 6 Things to Know About my Home on pages 94-95).

"I'm pretty sure that 10 minutes after my death my wife will hold a seance to ask me where the TV remote is."
(Rick Aaron, American anchor-man, reporter and producer.
Birth date unknown)

Your Business

You may have retired or been an employee during your working life rather than an owner. If so, you can skip this bit. However, if you own a business or a share in one, the content is extremely important. This brief treatment hardly does it justice and so further discussion with a solicitor will be needed, and those who inherit your business interests may well be very grateful to you.

Broadly, if you own all or part of a trading or indeed investment business (whether alone or as a partner) or if you own shares in a private limited company, you are very likely to need specific advice. This will be advice on (a) what happens to your business interest on your death and (b) ensuring you don't miss out on the Inheritance Tax reliefs.

If you are either a partner or a shareholder in an unlisted company, it is likely that the Partnership Agreement or a Shareholders' Agreement will specify what happens to the interest in the business on death. Typically, there will be 'pre-emption rights', under which the other partners or shareholders have a right within a specified period of time to buy out the deceased partner's/shareholder's interest at market value. Such a provision would usually take precedence over any gift under the Will.

In the case of a business which you own and run in entirety, there may be someone engaged in the business who you would like to take over after your death, maybe a son or daughter or an employee, typically by way of gift (rather than a sale/purchase). This needs careful planning, if not done already.

Also, consider what impact your death would have on the business and what would happen in the immediate aftermath. If, for the business to be able to continue, the contribution you have been making needs to be continued in someone else's hands, it may be appropriate to consider 'keyman' insurance. Such insurance covers that eventuality, to enable the business to hire the appropriate person at the appropriate salary over an appropriate period of time.

All these issues are matters you need to discuss with your business colleagues (if you have them), so that together you can make appropriate provision for anyone's unexpected death.

The other point to bear in mind in terms of Inheritance Tax is (at least, as at 1 November 2022) the likely availability of up to 100% relief from tax in the case of a trading (but not an investment) business (see page 62).

"One thing I've learned as I get older is just to go ahead and do it. It's much easier to apologise after something's been done than to get permission ahead of time."
(Grace Murray Hopper, American computer pioneer
and senior naval officer, 1906-1992)

Bank/Building Society Accounts and any Investments

Although cash accounts (whether current or deposit) in a bank or building society are different from Investments as a generic term (by which I mean stocks and shares or investment funds), they are inherently the same in kind. I deal with both together here and details of each can be listed in Appendix 5 (see page 91). This is because both bank/building society accounts and investments can be held either in sole names or joint names and, importantly, if in joint names, either as joint tenants or as tenants in common (see page 46 for the distinction).

The practical advantage of having at least a bank or a building society account in joint names is that the 'survivorship rule' applies. That is, the surviving name on the account can draw upon it simply on providing the death certificate to the bank or building society, as constituting proof of the death of the other joint owner. Especially if the first to die is the 'breadwinner', this can be an invaluable useful source of funds in the period before probate is obtained, i.e. alleviating financial worries.

In any event, details of the death should be given to every bank or building society with which you hold an account (with an official Death Certificate), as also the person who holds or manages the investments. The main point is that any bank or building society account which does not pass by survivorship is effectively 'frozen': no more payments can go in or out. Typically, the Executors will set up their own Executors' Bank Account into which on grant of probate will be paid the balances at your death of any bank or building society accounts.

Premium Bonds

Any Premium Bonds will form part of your Estate. Although prizes from Premium Bonds are not subject to tax, the value of Premium Bonds on death may attract Inheritance Tax. The Executors can straightforwardly sell the Bonds once probate has been granted and add the proceeds to the Executors' Account for distribution to the beneficiaries entitled. Alternatively, the Executors can choose to keep the Premium Bonds with National Savings & Investments (NS&I) for up to 12 months after death. If during that period any prizes are won, they could be claimed either by the Executors or by a nominated beneficiary. The Executors should ask the relevant beneficiary/ beneficiaries what to do.

If you own no more than £5,000 in Premium Bonds and National Savings Certificates combined, a grant of probate is not required before NS&I will distribute the value held on death[11]. If more than £5,000, probate is needed (if not also for other assets).

Insurance Policies

Insurance takes a variety of forms:
- life assurance
- property insurance
- contents/personal effects insurance
- car insurance
- 'permanent health' insurance
- private health insurance
- holiday cover insurance
- 'Keyman' business insurance.

Should your death trigger an insurance policy payout, e.g. a whole of life assurance or an endowment insurance policy (typically traditionally linked with a mortgage in the event of your death before a given age, tied to the length of the mortgage), then the policy will pay out on production of a death certificate, but not until the grant of probate. This is because the insurance company needs to be content that it will get a 'good receipt' from the Executors, who are thereby confirmed to be entitled to deal with your estate.

---

[11] Generally, see Appendix 7 Some Useful Resources on page 98 for a helpful website to consult on Premium Bonds.

On the other hand, if, as is ideally the case, the property has been written 'in trust', then the owner of the policy under the trust will receive the proceeds simply on production of a death certificate, assuming that the trust document has been provided to the insurance company. That could apply also in the event of your death on holiday under holiday cover. Typically, the proceeds of such a policy written in trust will not attract Inheritance Tax in your estate.

Otherwise, insurance being a contract between you and the insurance company, the latter needs to be informed, with details listed in Appendix 4 (page 88), and any regular premiums will, of course, stop.

"I took a physical for some life insurance. All they would give me was fire and theft."
(Milton Berle, American actor and comedian, 1908-2002)

Jewellery and other Valuables

You will have an idea of the value of these from your annual insurance policy. A market valuation will be needed as at the date of death, as with other property. You may choose to make particular bequests to favourite people (see page 29).

Your Car – and other Means of Transport

To this we might add e.g. motorbike, sailing dinghy or even yacht. If you have one, is it owned outright or subject to a hire purchase or lease agreement under which there should be cover written in for your death?

In the case of a car, DVLA will need to be informed, together with the identity of the new owner, as also will the insurers. Your driving licence will have to be surrendered to DVLA. Perhaps one of the family will take on your car or it will be sold.

Shotguns and Rifles (Firearms)

If you own a shotgun or a rifle (kept securely in a locked cabinet, whether at your home or elsewhere), you should think in advance about what is to happen on your death. The rule is that, unless the firearm is to be inherited by another family member who has their own licence and a key to the cabinet, it should be handed in to the police within 30 days after the death (or, perhaps, rather improbably as stated on the official website, an application made to have it kept 'as a souvenir'). The police will want to see both the death certificate and the firearms licence. Insurers should also be notified. If death seems imminent, this may be a good thing to sort out in advance.

Keys

These could be to house or flat (perhaps including a friend's/ neighbour's property) or doors within, to your car, safety deposit box, gates around the property or any number of other things. You may know what key opens what, but others might not. Keep your keys in a safe place(s) and properly labelled.

Collections of Particular Types of Property

You may not be a collector, but, if you are, have you thought about who should inherit? It could be stamps, books by a specific author, china, porcelain, paintings by a particular artist – or any number of things. Consider ensuring that the chosen recipient is aware of the background and is keen to preserve, and maybe indeed to add to, your collection – a topic for a conversation at least, if not also in writing. If the collection is of local or national importance and you want to ensure its preservation, you might like it to go to a museum. Again, a conversation can never be too early – and there may even be the possibility of an Inheritance Tax exemption for gifts to a heritage body, from what might be a considerable tax burden (depending upon market value). Don't be surprised if the answer is 'no', however, even for quite serious collections.

Photographs

You may be like or unlike me. Like me, if you have a few photograph albums of holidays and children growing up, with a myriad of other photographs, some in bundles and some scattered, with the full intention of 'someday' putting them in some sort of order. Unlike me, if you have already put all your photographs in order, neatly arranged book by book on a shelf – or, indeed, in the Cloud. This is just a reminder, if necessary, to do something about it – and, in particular, to chuck photographs which really are surplus to requirements, however tough that may be. Alternatively, you may have your photographs neatly ordered electronically, which is fine so long as your family can access them.

But the main point is this: thinking of 'old' photographs, that were perhaps taken even before you were born, which have a family interest, it is so important to have names and dates written on the back so that they can be identified.

"Half our life is spent trying to find something to do with the time we have rushed through life trying to save."
(Will Rogers, American vaudeville performer and
social commentator, 1879-1935)

Your Papers

By this I don't mean collections of letters and files (discussed below), but rather your papers (all, of course, meaningful, in some shape or form) however arranged, whether in your office, study or somewhere else. Once you are gone, it is likely that none of these will be of any relevance or interest to anybody else (with the odd exception). So it makes sense to do the culling process now, arranging for recycling - except in the case of very sensitive material which should be shredded or burnt. Perhaps keeping only that which, rigorously, you know you will need at some point.

"AND WHILE IT MIGHT MAKE SENSE TO HIM..."

Letters and Files

Many old files can be destroyed. Former Income Tax files, more than six years old, can generally be disposed of, unless advised otherwise by your accountant or tax agent (for example, in the case of an ongoing tax enquiry). That said, some files relating to the past may be of enduring interest to your family for the future, perhaps covering a past episode of your life when extraordinary things happened. But the mundane stuff can simply be binned.

Letters, if you do keep them, can be rather more sensitive and there are some of a personal nature which should be destroyed. If you do want to keep them, however, put them in a file with clear instructions given to your nearest and dearest to destroy (without 'peeking') after your death. Others, of more general family interest, you may wish to retain. At all events, do an inspection and sorting process.

Memoirs

Most of us will not write a published autobiography or even be so famous that someone else wishes to write a biography. However, whether or not you think that you have led an interesting life, your life will be precious to those you leave behind. While you might have 'told your tale' occasionally, it may well be that your family and those close to you would value some sort of account of your life, the people who have been important to you and, indeed, lessons you have learnt from life which you wish to pass on.

"Life isn't measured by how many breaths we take, but by the moments that take our breath away."
(Chinese saying)

Honours and Decorations

You may be the recipient of one of these, which you can record in Appendix 5 (see page 93). Note that, while some (most?) can be kept by the family, others are returnable. For example, the instructions inside a friend's MBE medal box state: "The Badge is not returnable on death and should be retained by the person legally entitled to receive it under the terms of the deceased's Will. Notification of the date of death of the recipient should be sent to the Secretary, Central Chancery of the Orders of Knighthood, St. James's Palace, London SW1A 1BH." By contrast, "Some insignia of the greater Orders are returnable on death."[12]

---

[12] Words taken from a booklet entitled 'The Investitures' produced by British Ceremonial Arts Ltd.

CHAPTER 5

YOUR PLANS FOR THE FUTURE
Thinking them Through

"Find a life worth enjoying; take risks; love deeply; have no regrets; and always, always have rebellious hope."
(Dame Deborah James, English cancer campaigner and podcast host, 1981-2022)

Setting the Scene

A doctor friend of mine, who worked in palliative care, told me that a solicitor was asked by the family of one of her patients to come and draw up a Will. The patient was extremely unwell and likely to die within a few days. He was semi-conscious and receiving high dose diamorphine. The solicitor had gone to see the patient, then came to ask my friend if she could say he was 'of sound mind'. She could not, in all honesty, confirm that, if the Will was contested in court, she could *"take the witness stand and state that the patient fully understood his intentions, given his poor condition"*. As a result, whenever she saw a patient for the first time, after the clinical issues were discussed, my doctor friend would always recommend that they get their affairs in order, including their Will.

"Write, paint, sculpt, learn the piano, take up dancing, whether it is the tango or line dancing, start a college course, fall in love all over again – the possibilities are limitless for you to achieve your private ambitions."
(Dame Joan Collins, English actress, author and columnist, 1933 -   )

Inheritance Tax

Inheritance Tax (also known as 'death duties') describes tax on capital which passes on death. In one sense, it might seem quite surprising to find a section on taxation in a Book such as this. However, 'old habits die hard', my having advised, lectured on and written about tax professionally for 35 years. This is far from a complete guide, so get specialist advice, perhaps from your solicitor when drawing up your Will or from your accountant, or even both. Be aware that there are certain exemptions which apply during your lifetime but not on death. So, if used properly, they can reduce the size of your taxable estate on death.

The General Rule on Death

Subject to the exemption for gifts to a surviving spouse/civil partner, the value of your Estate is totted up. That includes any chargeable gifts made in the seven years before you die, at their then-value. If you do not have a United Kingdom domicile (which is the country where you have made your permanent home), then, broadly speaking, only property within the United Kingdom attracts Inheritance Tax. However, even if you are domiciled outside the UK under the general law, you will still be treated as domiciled within the UK for Inheritance Tax purposes if you have been resident here for at least 15 out of the previous 20 tax years - or if you have been domiciled in the UK within the three years before your death.

The first £325,000 (the 'nil-rate band') of your Estate is free of tax, with the balance charged at 40%. This is subject to 'tapering relief' on the rate of tax charged, where the gift exceeded the nil-rate band of £325,000 and more than three years have passed since the date it was made. In addition, there is an allowance of £350,000 for a residence per married couple/civil partnership (£175,000 per individual) which can be used either on the first or on the second death. To the extent that the nil-rate band is not used on the first death, the unused percentage can be passed on to the second.

Any Inheritance Tax which is payable becomes due on the last day of the month falling six months after that in which death occurred. In practice, except in very straightforward cases, this is unlikely to happen. If the application for Probate shows Tax as payable, it must be paid (typically through a bank loan, if not by the residuary beneficiaries) before Probate will be granted. Very often an initial estimate of Tax will be finalised by agreement with HMRC when the Estate is wound up.

A brief word about the complete exemption from Inheritance Tax for gifts to a spouse or civil partner. It applies equally to lifetime gifts and inheritances following a death. The exemption is limited to £325,000 for gifts from a UK domiciled person to a spouse/civil partner who is not UK domiciled. However, this exemption applies only in cases where the couple are legally married or are registered civil partners. It is a common misapprehension among those who otherwise live together (however long and stable the relationship) that on the first death, in the absence of a Will, the survivor inherits everything and that, whether or not there is a Will, there is an exemption from Inheritance Tax. Both views are mistaken (see page 25).

"If you were going to die soon and had only one phone call you could make, who would you call and what would you say? And why are you waiting?"
(Stephen Levine, American poet, author and teacher, 1937-2016)

The Lifetime Exemptions

•   Potentially Exempt Transfers (PETs). These are gifts to an individual which the donor survives for seven years, in which case it becomes exempt.   Death within that period brings the consequence described on page 59. A gift must be absolute, that is the donor must enjoy (or 'reserve') no benefit from it. Payment of a full market 'rent' (which should continue until death) prevents a benefit arising[12].

•   The Annual Exemption. Gifts of £3,000 in total (to one or more people) in a tax year (6 April to 5 April) are exempt. To the extent that the allowance is unused, it can be carried forward for one year only. The annual exemption could be used for gifts in cash or perhaps to pay premiums on a life assurance policy written in trust for others or even to make gifts in kind – a painting worth up to £3,000 for example. Alternatively, it could be used to create or to add to a stakeholder pension for a child or grandchild: a payment of £2,880 (net of 20% basic rate tax, i.e. £3,600 gross, to which the Government will add the tax of £720) can be made for a minor beneficiary or indeed an adult.

---

[12] See the family tale on page 44 for an illustration of how this might work.

- The £250 small gifts exemption. A gift of up to £250 (but no more) to any individual in a tax year is exempt. Note that this exemption can't be used in conjunction with the £3,000 annual exemption. So a gift of £3,250 to a particular individual will be covered by the annual exemption of £3,000 and as to £250 (if not within the normal expenditure out of income exemption – see below) will be a PET.

- Normal expenditure out of income. A transfer will be exempt if (taking one year with another) it was made out of income leaving the donor with sufficient net income to maintain his/her usual standard of living, that is without resort to capital. To establish this, a pattern of giving should be started as early as possible, with records kept to back up any claim.

- The marriage/civil partnership exemption. When a person gets married or enters into a civil partnership, the exemption depends on the relationship between donor and donee:
  - £5,000 per parent (or step-parent)
  - £2,500 per grandparent (or step-grandparent)
  - £1,000 for all others.
  A gift may be in kind as well as in cash. The gift must be an outright gift – and the exemption will not apply if the nuptials are called off.

Reliefs & Exemptions applying both to lifetime gifts and on death

- The spouse/ civil partner exemption: see pages 59-60.

- The charities exemption. This exemption applies to gifts on death just as to lifetime gifts. However, one advantage of a lifetime gift is the possibility of Income Tax relief for Gift Aid: both basic rate recovery for the charity and higher rate relief for the donor. So a charitably (and tax-saving) minded person, who is a higher rate taxpayer, might on their deathbed be advised to make a gift to one or more charities before they die rather than under their Will, provided they pay in that tax year enough Income Tax or Capital Gains Tax to 'frank' the tax recovery by the charity.[13]

---

[13] See the alternative suggestion of achieving both Inheritance Tax and Income Tax efficiency through a post-death Deed of Variation, on page 32.

- Reliefs for agricultural and business property. Subject to particular conditions, an interest in a trading business is likely to attract 100% Business Property Relief on market value in computing Inheritance Tax. If the business is a farm, a mix of Agricultural Property Relief and Business Property Relief may well apply. The reliefs apply equally with lifetime gifts, though there is then an additional condition that, should either donor (the giver) or donee (the recipient) die within the seven years, the donee must still have retained at that point either the original or qualifying replacement property and that (very broadly speaking) it would still qualify for relief in his or her hands, under the 'claw-back' rule.

There is also (1 November 2022, at least[14]) a very favourable Capital Gains Tax rule which means that a gift of such a property on death is preferable in overall tax terms to a lifetime gift. This is because of the general rule on death that any inherent capital gain in the property is effectively 'washed' and taken out of charge to tax, with the new owner inheriting at the then market value. So, in the case of agricultural and business property, there is a 'double whammy' in terms of achieving both 100% relief from Inheritance Tax and the disappearance of any inherent chargeable gain in the property. This type of relief needs detailed professional advice and may very easily be restricted in a future Budget.

Religious Faith

While possibly not a subject you would expect to find in a practical guide to putting your affairs in order, it is important for everyone, at least, to consider. This is not just because I am an ordained minister in the Church of England. Whatever your religious background, or none, there comes a time when any beliefs (or lack of them) you hold can usefully be questioned, even if you remain of the same mind.

Certainly, I have found that the prospect of death is a time when people want to rethink these things.

Of course, you may be what one might call 'actively religious' and your faith may well become increasingly important to you as the end draws

---

[14] I must emphasise that this section (like everything else in this Book) must not be taken as advice.

nigh. Alternatively, if you have no faith or spiritual belief and believe that death is the end, you may wish to consider if that is indeed the case for you. Or, if you do have a religious faith background (whether Christian, Jewish, Muslim, Hindu, Buddhist, Sikh, Mormon or Jehovah's Witness or something else), but haven't made it an especially important part of your life, now might be a good time to talk to a spiritual guide or trusted friend to explore what that faith means for you and those around you.

It may touch on the way you pass your remaining time and, indeed, the arrangements you make for your funeral.

"I do benefits for all religions. I'd hate to blow the hereafter on a technicality."
(Bob Hope, British-American comedian and actor, 1903-2003)

Downsizing (House or Flat)

You may already be living in a house or flat, whether you own or rent it, out of which you would like to be 'carried in your coffin'. If not, there may come a time when it makes sense to move, occasioned perhaps by declining health or the general impact of ageing, or the house and particularly the garden may have become too big for you to manage. In any case, think about it before the need arises. You may wish to move nearer one or more of your children, if they are not close by already. The timing might depend on a range of things, including the property market and the availability of suitable replacement accommodation.

If you own your home, this might be an opportunity to unlock some capital, perhaps to make gifts to your children or grandchildren. Moving from two or more storeys to a single storey could make sense, maybe with a walk-in/wheel-in wet room instead of a more conventional bathroom. Adaptation or adaptability of appliances of one sort or another could be useful, along with things like doorways wide enough for wheelchairs, positioning switches etc.

Downsizing will almost inevitably mean the need to 'get rid of' furniture, books and other things surplus to requirements, whether to children or an auction house, if not (sadly) the skip.

"I'M SORRY MARK BUT YOU'RE ALSO PART OF THE DECLUTTERING PROCESS."

Finances

Here I want to give a general warning that you should not give too much away too soon. You could be motivated by generosity, in wanting to see your family helped financially or even in terms of Inheritance Tax mitigation (see pages 60-62). That said, however, old age has a habit of being expensive in terms of personal care and/or care homes if needed. So think very carefully before giving money away, for example released by the sale of a more expensive home when downsizing, in terms of what your future needs might be. If there are two of you, do bear in mind the future needs of the survivor of you, especially if there may be many years to consider and provide for.

Places you Want to Visit/Things to Do

I have on my bookshelf *A Thousand Places to See before You Die*, by Patricia Schultz (referenced in Appendix 7 on page 98). The vast majority of these places I would yet like to visit I won't manage. However, I have found it quite fun to check the book before taking a foreign holiday.

Anyway, the adage 'What you don't want to be saying on your death bed' does prompt the question as to places you would like to visit or things you would like to do while you still have the physical and mental capacity – and, indeed, the money – to do so.

"Twenty years from now you will be more disappointed by the things that you didn't do than by the ones you did do. So throw off the bowlines. Sail away from the safe harbor. Catch the trade winds in your sails. Explore. Dream. Discover."
(H. Jackson Brown Jr., American author, 1940-2021)

CHAPTER 6

POST-SCRIPT
What Happens Afterwards

"The pain passes, but the beauty remains"
(Pierre-Auguste Renoir, French artist, 1841-1919)

Setting the Scene

The content of this section will come as no surprise. Just as every deceased is individual, so is the impact on those they leave behind. Yes, grieving can be collective, but, where a relationship was close, it will be intensely personal. So this is a message both for those who are left and for those who are close to them (whether or not also close to the one who has died).

Grief has no overall 'descriptor', nor indeed a timetable. People grieve differently. In many ways the loss will be with the bereaved until the day they die – and the impact will come and go in different ways and at different times. But life does go on, though it will never be the same. We need to recognise that, both for ourselves and for others, with care, love and sensitivity: 'self-care' is both essential and not selfish. The AtaLoss website referenced in Appendix 7 on page 98 is a useful resource for bereaved people and those supporting them, in providing a signpost to information and services.

For the funeral, see pages 19-21.

"I've learned that people will forget what you said, people will forget what you did, but people will never forget how you made them feel."
(Maya Angelou, American memoirist, poet and civil rights activist, 1928-2014)

Notifications

You, as well as your nearest and dearest, will need to have in mind what can best be described as a 'process' (though that is a sadly impersonal word) which will kick in on death.

It starts with telling people the sad news, best in person if possible, though, if not, by telephone. Here you will have made two lists:

- first, family and close friends to tell personally – and some trusted friends and
- second, those to email, which would include advisers and a variety of contacts, including insurance companies etc.

Both lists can be compiled and kept up-to-date, by adapting the pro forma in Appendix 4 (see pages 88-89).

One important notification – and contact to be made as soon as reasonably practicable – is to the chosen funeral directors (see page 88).

Obtaining the Death Certificate

The Death Certificate is confirmation of registration of a death in the UK. The applicant will need[15]:

- A medical certificate of the cause of death, signed by a doctor, typically in the hospital or nursing home, or the GP if death occurs at home
- Details of any State Pension or other Benefits being paid at the date of death
- Birth Certificate
- Council Tax Bill
- Driving Licence
- Passport
- Marriage/Civil Partnership Certificate where applicable.

Production of the above documents is not essential, though the information given within them must be produced.

The General Register Office (GRO) has a two-page application form which most easily is completed online. The application form has five sections:

- Applicant (or 'customer') details
- Details of death
- GRO index reference
- Other information (including number of Certificates required)
- Payment information.

---

[15] Generally, see the website referenced in Appendix 7 (on page 99) for How to go about getting the Death Certificate.

The family do need to be quick in registering a death: up to five days are allowed in England, Wales or Northern Ireland, whereas it is eight days in Scotland. Instead of initiating the process online, you could make an appointment at the local Register Office. Typically, the registration is done by a close relative. The Registrar will also want to know if any benefits were being received at the date of death, including pensions.

In cases where there is a sudden or unexpected death, a Coroner (or Procurator Fiscal in Scotland) may be appointed to investigate the circumstances of the death, both for official purposes and to provide some understanding (if not comfort) to family and friends.

HM Government's 'Tell Us Once' Service

This is an extraordinarily useful service about which the Registrar will tell the person registering your death. The Registrar will either complete the Tell Us Once service with them or give them a unique reference number, so they can use the service themselves (whether online or by telephone, within 28 days after getting the unique reference number). To use the service the person registering your death will need: your name, date of birth, address, date of death, name, address and contact details of the Executor(s), details of the surviving spouse/civil partner, failing which their next of kin and, if you died in a hospital, nursing home, care home or hospice, its name and address. They may also need: your passport number and town of birth, driving licence number, vehicle registration numbers of any vehicles owned, name of your local council and any benefits being received, plus details of any Armed Forces or public sector pension schemes to which payments were being made or payments were being received.

Tell Us Once will contact all of: HMRC; DWP; the Passport Office; DVLA; the Local Council; Veterans UK; Social Security Scotland, together with any relevant public sector pensions schemes. All the details can be found on: www.gov.uk/after-a-death/organisations-you-need-to-contact-and-tell-us-once.

My old Mam read the obituary column every day, but she could never understand how people always die in alphabetical order."
(Frank Carson, Northern Irish actor, 1926-2012)

Newspaper Announcement(s)

If going in one or more national newspapers (The Times, The Daily Telegraph, The Guardian etc), as well as any local newspapers, this can be quite expensive. So, bear in mind that the cost is a deductible expense for Inheritance Tax purposes. You could suggest where announcements could be placed and even draft a form of words, e.g. SURNAME, first or full personal names, date of death and age, names of close relatives left behind and (if known) any funeral arrangements.

There's a joke about a lady whose husband dies and she rings up the local newspaper to announce his passing. She is given three words for free, so she chooses 'Fred is dead'. The newspaper is horrified and so gives her another three words for free. In the newspaper the next day, the announcement reads 'Fred is dead, Volvo for sale.'

Headstone

You might also like to suggest some content for a headstone in a churchyard (bearing in mind the disciplines applied on wording by the Church of England or by the Parish Priest) or perhaps for a memorial stone where ashes may be scattered on property owned by you or by one of the family.

"I told you I was ill."
(Spike Milligan KBE, Irish comic, actor, musician and poet, 1918 – 2002)

Accessing and Implementing the Will and any Letters of Wishes

As well as leaving your latest Will and any Letters of Wishes with your solicitors, you may have given copies to each of your Executors, though this would be unusual. At the same time, to avoid any surprises, you may wish to tell family members of the broad terms of your Will. And, especially in the event of distribution of any chattels or personal possessions, create some system of distribution between those you leave behind, so it can be seen as 'fair' and to avoid any unnecessary squabbles (see page 44 for a suggestion). While 'the business' of reading through and implementing the provisions of your Will can await the funeral, it might be sensible for those close to you to have notice of anything in it or any Letters of Wishes which touch on funeral arrangements: you wouldn't want them to have had the cremation only to find out later you wanted to be buried ... (see pages 19-21).

"THEY DIDN'T SPECIFY SO WE DECIDED TO COVER BOTH BASES."

The Probate Procedure

The Grant of Probate is made to the named Executors in the Will. It is the authority of the Court to the Executors that they can 'administer' your Estate. Assuming that the Estate is liable for Inheritance Tax (see page 59), the application for Probate is in effect a notification for Inheritance Tax purposes. While this needs to be done within 12 months after the end of the month in which death occurs, it may well take up to most or even all of that time in complex cases. Even relatively straightforward cases can take between three and six months before the Executors or the solicitors are ready to make the application. Until Probate is granted, the Executors do not have the authority to deal with the assets of the Estate or pay off liabilities. Any money coming in after death will be paid into an Executors' Account, typically managed by the solicitors.

So, the more up-to-date you can keep your list of possessions (Appendix 5 on pages 91-93), the easier their task will be. This should include any liabilities.

The application for Probate will be accompanied by the appropriate fee, which is value related.

If the Estate is liable for Inheritance Tax, application cannot be made for Probate until the Inheritance Tax Forms have been sent to HMRC and at least 20 working days have elapsed.

"Death is no more than passing from one room to another.
But there's a difference to me, you know . Because in that other room
I shall be able to see."
(Helen Keller, blind American author, disability rights advocate and lecturer, 1880-1968)

Moving Forward

The administration of the Estate will be complete once the Executors have paid the Inheritance Tax due, paid off all the other liabilities and distributed the assets or their proceeds of sale. There are two qualifications to this:

- Inheritance Tax on some assets (most commonly, land and buildings) may be payable by interest-bearing instalments over a period of 10 years; and
- especially where minor children are involved, there might be a continuing trust whether of residue or of part of the Estate, in which case Trustees will look after that, who may be the same individuals as the Executors, albeit now in a different capacity. That trust will have to be registered with HMRC for tax purposes and a new process begun (see pages 28-29).

Then, again with minor children, guardians will ideally have been named in the Will who, once both parents have died, will take over legal and pastoral responsibility for the children. They will ideally be given the financial wherewithal to enable them to do that, all in accordance with your Letter of Wishes.

In a major sense, death is not the end, in that the grieving process continues for those you have left behind. But you can make it easier for them in particular, by leaving your affairs in order, the subject-matter of *Your Last Gift*, and by giving any help that might be appropriate to enable them to 'move forward'.

THE APPENDICES

Appendices 1 to 6 form the practical element of this Book. As stated on page 21, purchase of the book will enable you to access the secure part of the website www.yourlastgiftbook.com.

You can adapt the various forms to your own circumstances, whether for electronic use on your own computer or to be printed out to create your own master documents. And in either case to be stored securely. The purpose of including Appendices 1 to 6 in the Book is to alert you to what you will find on the website, to make the forms your own.

APPENDIX 1.1

CRITICAL CHECKLIST

1. Who to Tell of the Death

Who are the first people who need to know, in order of priority (including my Executors)?

Address	Name	Relationship	Telephone	Email

2. Guardians for minor children

If I have children under the age of 18, have I and my spouse/ partner thought about appointing testamentary guardians?	Yes	Date	Yet to Do	Pages in Book 11, 16, 73

3. Pets

Description, name, age	Any particular features or characteristics?	Microchip ID

Who is to look after my domestic animals in the short term?

	Name	Telephone	Email	Address
Dogs				
Cats				
Horses				
Other				

Have I made arrangements for someone to look after my pet(s)/domestic animals in the long term after my death?

Yes	Date	Yet to do	Pages in Book
			11,16

Is there an insurance policy in place of which they should be aware? If so, details?

Yes	Date	Yet to do	Page in Book
			16

Vet details

Animal	Vet name	Telephone	Email	Address
Dogs				
Cats				

4. Access to cash (joint accounts)

How can my surviving spouse/civil partner get cash for ongoing expenses?

A/C Details	Sort code	Account No	Pages in Book
			11,49

5. Passwords (and see Appendix 4 for Digital Assets on page 93)

Where are my passwords?

	Location	Page in Book
Passwords		11
Safe Key		11
Digital Devices		17-19
Password Manager		18
Others		17-19

6. Where is my Will?

	Location	Page in Book
		30

7. Registering my death: where are my certificates which provide the necessary information?

	Location	Page in Book
		69

APPENDIX 1.2

COMPREHENSIVE CHECKLIST

1. My Will

	Yes	Date	Yet to Do	Pages in Book
Have I made it, properly witnessed and dated?				26-33
Is my Will up-to-date, in terms of: - my choice of Executors/Guardians - my wishes - property owned - beneficiaries alive?				27-29 29, 30, 45 29 29
Have I written any appropriate Letters of Wishes? Do those Letters of Wishes properly reflect my current intentions?				30
Have I stored it/them for safe-keeping? Where?				30
Have I invited and informed my named Executors?				27
If my Will provides for a continuing trust (perhaps to provide for minor children), have I made any necessary arrangements for the administration and running of that trust, including Letters of Wishes?				28-29

2. Accessing and Implementing the Will and any Letters of Wishes

	Yes	Date	Yet to Do	Page in Book
Do my Executors know where my last Will and any Letters of Wishes are stored for safekeeping?				30
Have I destroyed any previous Wills made which are not current?				27
Have I told family members of the broad terms of the Will, to avoid any unwelcome surprises?				72

3. Obtaining the Death Certificate

	Yes	Date	Yet to Do	Pages in Book
Have I thought about who might do this and agreed it with them? See Critical Checklist point 7.				69-70

4. Funeral Arrangements

	Yes	Date	Yet to Do	Pages in Book
Have I told my nearest and dearest of my wish to be buried or cremated – and where?				19-21
Have I chosen my preferred Funeral Directors and told my Executors?				19
Have I decided on a religious funeral or secular ceremony and written down my wishes on what and who should be involved?				19-21
Have I considered the possibility of a memorial service or event some months after my death?				21
Will the cost of the above be easily met from my cash resources?				19-21
Have I discussed with my nearest and dearest what sort of wake I would like to be held?				21
Have I taken out a funeral plan? If so, details?				19-20

5. Post-Death Notifications

	Yes	Date	Yet to Do	Pages in Book
Have I made a list of people to contact (Appendix 4)?				75, 88-89

6. Newspaper Announcements

	Yes	Date	Yet to Do	Page in Book
Have I considered where an announcement should be placed and even drafted some suggested wording?				71

7. Headstone/Memorial Stone

	Yes	Date	Yet to Do	Page in Book
Have I suggested some preferred wording for a Headstone in a churchyard or for a Memorial Stone where my ashes will be scattered on my or a family member's property?				71

8. Records of Information

	Yes	Date	Yet to Do	Pages in Book
Have I completed and stored: • Personal Details (Appendix 2) • Important Documents – Whereabouts (Appendix 3) • People to Contact (Appendix 4) • List of Possessions (Appendix 5) • Things to Know About my Home (Appendix 6) and told those close to me where these records may be accessed?				86 87 88-89 91-93 94-95

9. Lasting Powers of Attorney (LPA)

	Yes	Date	Yet to Do	Pages in Book
Have I made a Lasting Power of Attorney: - Property and Financial Affairs? - Health and Welfare?				11-14
Has my LPA been registered with the Office of the Public Guardian?				12

10. Medical Treatment

	Yes	Date	Yet to Do	Page in Book
Have I written an 'advance decision' which my Health and Welfare Attorney can give to a hospital or other medical person? Or a RESPECT form?				14 15

11. Dealing with House Contents

	Yes	Date	Yet to Do	Page in Book
Have I arranged with someone to remove and deal with my possessions after my death?				46

12. Organ Donation

	Yes	Date	Yet to Do	Page in Book
If I don't want any of my organs in good working order at my death to be donated, have I recorded my decision on the NHS Organ Donor Register?				34

13. Gifts

	Yes	Date	Yet to Do	Page in Book
Have I thought of making gifts now to especially favourite people?				40

14. If I am involved in owning and/or running a business

	Yes	Date	Yet to Do	Pages in Book
Have I considered and made arrangements (perhaps with others) as to how the business can continue successfully after my death or incapacity?				47-48
Have I made appropriate provision under my Will for the inheritance of the sole trade/partnership share/ company shares?				48
If necessary, have I considered and made arrangements for appropriate 'keyman' insurance to hire in a new employee to replace me (for whatever period of time)?				48
Have I gathered together and left in a safe and accessible place all the documentation relating to my business interests which my successor(s) will need, including any expressed wishes and observations which will help my successor in dealing with my business interests?				48

15. Letters to Family and Friends

	Yes	Date	Yet to Do	Page in Book
Have I considered writing (or updating) a letter to one or more especially favourite family member or friends?				39
Have I left clear instructions with my Executors as to where those letters are and how they will be delivered after my death?				39

16. Relationships

	Yes	Date	Yet to Do	Page in Book
Have I done what I can to mend any that are 'broken', so that I have no 'unfinished business' with anyone?				40

17. Destruction of useless or sensitive papers etc

	Yes	Date	Yet to Do	Page in Book
Have I taken steps to dispose of or destroy any papers, letters or files which either are of no use to me now or which would be of no possible interest after my death or which may be sensitive?				53

18. Memoirs

	Yes	Date	Yet to Do	Page in Book
Have I thought about writing for those I leave behind some story of my life which they might like to have?				55

19. Inheritance Tax

	Yes	Date	Yet to Do	Pages in Book
Have I taken steps to estimate any Inheritance Tax payable on my death and made financial provision for payment?				58-62
Have I thought about using the 'lifetime exemptions' to reduce the potential burden of Inheritance Tax, whether through gifts to individuals or donations to charity?				60-62
Have I put together a list of significant gifts made in the last seven years?				45,59

20. Downsizing and decluttering

	Yes	Date	Yet to Do	Pages in Book
Have I considered (with anyone with whom I live) for how long I might want to stay in my present home?				63-64
If appropriate, have I discussed with those close to me where I might move – and where? And when?				63-64
Have I started the process of decluttering?				64

21. Places to Visit/Things To Do

	Yes	Date	Yet to Do	Page in Book
Have I considered places I might yet like to visit or things to do?				65

22. Secure Storage

	Yes	Date	Yet to Do	Page in Book
Have I made arrangements for safe deposit of all the information which my family and Executors will need following my death – and easy access by them when the time comes?				6

APPENDIX 2

PERSONAL DETAILS

Surname	
First name(s)	
Any other names (by which known) e.g. maiden name	
Relationship status: single/married/civil partnership/widowed/divorced	
Address (if rented, name and contact details of landlord and/or agent)	
Telephone no(s) – Landline & Mobile	
Email address(es)	
Spouse/partner name and contact details	
If different, next-of-kin name, address and telephone and contact details	
Work status: employed/self-employed/unemployed/retired/other	
Occupation/profession (whether former or active)	
Place and name of work, with address and telephone and email contact details	
Employer's PAYE reference	
VAT registration number	
Date of Birth	
Place of Birth	
National Insurance No	
NHS No	
Tax Reference No (UTR)	
Passport No	
Driving Licence No	
Religion or Spiritual Belief - and (where relevant) denomination/branch	
Licence Nos (e.g. Firearms, Shotgun, Pilot, Yacht Captain's Certificate)	
Military Service (Service No, rank and any decorations)	
Post-nominal Letters (honours and decorations)	
Health: Doctor's surgery (name, address, email and telephone no.)/ Blood Group/Allergies/Phobias/Medication/Dietary Requirements/ Disabilities (Physical or Mental)	

WHEREABOUTS OF IMPORTANT DOCUMENTS

Type	Reference	Location
Advance Direction (expression of health wishes at the end of life)		
RESPECT FORM (Recommended Summary Plan for Emergency Care and Treatment)		
Power(s) of Attorney		
Will & Letters of Wishes		
Funeral Plan Details		
Funeral Wishes		
Birth Certificate		
Marriage/Civil Partnership/ Divorce/Dissolution Certificates		
Change of Name Certificate		
Passport		
House or Flat/Land Certificates		
Building Society Passbooks		
Bank Statements		
Driving Licence		
Car Registration Log Book(s)		
MOT Certificate(s)		
TV Licence		
Insurance Certificates		
Business papers		
Tax Papers		
Pension Papers		
Annuity Papers		
Shotgun Certificate, Firearms Licence		
Loan and Finance Agreements		
Credit/Debit Cards		
Share Certificates		
Password details		

APPENDIX 4

PEOPLE TO CONTACT

	Name	Telephone	Email	Address
Family and friends (with relationship) - and whether they are your, or you are their, attorney				
Funeral Directors				
Vicar or other Religious Leader				
Doctor				
Dentist				
Business colleagues				
Solicitors				
Accountants				
Financial Advisers				
Land Agents/Surveyors				
Landlord of Rented Property				
Mortgage Company				
Occupation/profession:				
Insurance Company/Companies -				
- Life Insurance				
- Property Insurance				
- Contents/Personal Effects Insurance				
- Car Insurance				
- Holiday Cover Insurance				
- Permanent Health Insurance				
- Private healthcare insurance				
- 'Keyman' Business Insurance				
DWP for State Pension				
Private Pension Providers				

Organisations, including Clubs, Associations or Societies to which I belong

	Name	Individual	Ref .No	Email
Tell Us Once (see page 70)				
DVLA (Driving Licence)				
Blue Badge				
Travel Cards (rail/bus)				
Library Cards				
Passport				
If Lasting Power of Attorney made, Office of Public Guardian (see page 12)				
Police (for firearms - see page 52)				
Medals and Honours (see page 55)				

Companies of which I am an Officer and Trusts (whether family or charitable) of which I am a Trustee and active Deceased Estates where I am an Executor, plus people who are still alive who I know have appointed me as an Executor.

Description	Name	Number	My Responsibility	Contact Name	Email

See Appendix 6 for House-related Services and Contacts

APPENDIX 5

LIST OF POSSESSIONS

Property

Address	Solely / Jointly owned	Freehold/ leasehold (and if leasehold details of landlord)	Mortgaged?	Estimated Gross Value (before mortgage)

Cash/savings

Bank/Building Society	Name	Ac/no	Sort Code	Address	Approximate Balance

Regular Payments into my account(s) (one group per recipient bank account)

Type	Regularity	Amount	Reference	Contact details

Finance Cards

Bank/Company	Description	Card No.

Investments and other Financial Assets
(ISA's, Shares/Unit Trusts, Fixed Interest Bonds, Premium Bonds, Pension Funds)

Name	Approx Value	Manager Name & Individual Contact	Email	Address	Telephone

Insurance Policies paying out on my death (whether or not written in trust)

Company	Approx Value	Number	Contact	Email	Address	Telephone	Payable to

Liabilities (Mortgages and Monies Owed. Guarantor of Loans?)

Bank/ Lender	Account/ Roll No.	Amount	Period of loan	Date of loan	Amount Outstanding

Direct Debits & Standing Orders (including subscriptions)

DD/SO	Amount	From which account	Payee	Frequency	Date of payment

Chattels (Household items, Personal effects, Other)

Item	Approximate Value	My chosen recipient (under Will or Letter of Wishes)

High Value Items (Cars, Boats, Interests in Trusts, Works of Art, Jewellery, Shotguns, Rifles etc)

Item	Approximate Value	My chosen recipient (under Will or Letter of Wishes)

Business Interests (including Farms and Woodlands)

Item	Business Structure (Sole trade/partnership/ company)	Approximate value	Chosen recipient/main contact	Other details (eg pre-emption rights, insurances etc)

Online Accounts

Account	Description	Any Reference	Contact details	Means of access

Technology & Digital Assets

Devices	Description	Serial No's	Access to passwords/ Password Manager	Security question and answer
PC				
Mobile Phone				
Ipad				

Social Media Accounts

Account	Description	Any Reference	Access to passwords/ Password Manager	Security question and answer
Facebook				
Twitter				
Instagram				

Other Facilities

Account	Description	Any Reference	Access to passwords / Password Manager	Security question and answer
Dropbox				
Crypto Currency				
Email				

Other Possessions (Loans owed to me, Collections of particular types of property, photographs, medals)

Item	Details	My chosen recipient (under Will or Letter of Wishes)

APPENDIX 6
THINGS TO KNOW ABOUT MY HOME

Address	
Phone Number	
Owned or Rented?	
Keys: Location and what they open	

Utilities

Type	Supplier	Reference No.	Email	Telephone	Address
Electricity					
Gas					
Water					
Alarm					
Council Tax					
Landline telephone					
Mobile telephone					
Internet					
Satellite TV					
Security: CCTV					
Solar Panels					

Help in and around the House

Business Type	Name	Email	Telephone	Address
Electrician				
Gas Engineer				
Plumber				
Cleaner				
Window Cleaner				
"Handyman"				
Locksmith				
Gardener				

Maintenance Contracts

Description	Reference	Name	Email	Telephone
Alarm System				
CCTV				
Computer Installations				
Boiler				

Insurance (Property and Contents)

Type	Company/ Broker	Ref No.	Email	Telephone	Address

Where things are

Description	Location
Alarm System Box	
Fuse Box	
"Hiding Places" for valuables etc	
Meter: electricity	
Meter: gas	
Meter: water	
Stopcock(s)	
Safe(s) & access code(s) / keys	

APPENDIX 7
SOME USEFUL RESOURCES

Books

Butler, Larry and Templeton, Sheila, Edited by, *Living Our Dying* **(Rymour Books, 2021)**
This book brings together a wide range of offerings, both prose and poetry. These include reflections and personal testimonies contributed by 32 authors. Intended to inform people more deeply about dying, it is an attempt to overcome what is traditionally a taboo subject.

Clarke, Rachel, *Dear Life: A Doctor's Story of Love, Loss and Consolation* **(Thomas Dunne Books, 2020)**
A very powerful treatment of the end of life by palliative care specialist Dr Rachel Clarke. While unmistakably professional, the book is very personal, in particular about the author's relationship with her father who had inspired her to become a doctor and was then himself diagnosed with terminal cancer. It is a moving journey of a doctor, who is also a daughter and indeed a human being, intended to help those in the last stages of life.

Duncan Rogers, Jane, *Before I Go: The Essential Guide to Creating a Good End of Life Plan* **(Findhorn Press, 2018)**
This book is a very practical guide on how each one of us can take steps to ensure that our wants are being looked after at the end of our lives and after our death. The author doctor lost her own husband in 2011 (seven years before the book was published). Over one third of the content deals with the subject of preparation for the exercise, including addressing the subject of death. The major part deals with the recording of practical information for those we leave behind, as well as our wishes during the last days and post-death. There is a related website.

Gawande, Atul, *Being Mortal, Illness, Medicine and What Matters in the End* **(Profile Books, 2014)**
This book, which I read after hearing Atul Gawande deliver the Reith Lectures in 2014, is a powerful reflection by a US physician about mortality. A very personal account, it was the author's experience of looking after patients on the ward, listening to and responding to their concerns which changed his own views about life. To quote the fly sheet, it is *"about the modern experience of mortality – about what it is like to get old and die, how medicine has changed this and how it hasn't, where ideas about death have gone wrong"*.

Hutton, Deborah, *What Can I Do to Help? 75 Practical Ideas for Family and Friends from Cancer's Frontline* **(Short Books, 2005)**
An extraordinary book written by my late sister Debbie during the last eight months of her life between diagnosis of Stage 4 cancer and death. She describes what she calls the cancer club as *"the only club I can think of which is both rigorously exclusive and which has no*

waiting list, ever". It is a very well written collection of 75 practical suggestions to help family and friends suffering with cancer, drawing on interviews which journalist Debbie did with a variety of high-profile people.

Lewis, C.S., *A Grief Observed* (Faber & Faber, 1961)
Best-known as the author of the Narnia books, C.S. Lewis was an academic and Christian writer. After the tragic death of his wife in 1960, Lewis wrote this *"reflection on how in the midst of bereavement we might think about the most important issues of life, of death and of faith"*, as he sought to come to terms with grief.

Morgan, Pamela, *Cryptoasset Inheritance Planning: A Simple Guide for Owners* (TPF, 2021)
A step-by-step guide about owning cryptocurrency tokens, crypto-collectables and other cryptoassets and what happens to these assets when you die. Within the book, there are checklists, templates and worksheets to help the reader to create their inheritance plan. While written within the context of US law and practice, the book can apply to cryptoassets wherever situated in the world, subject, of course, to getting legal advice in the appropriate jurisdiction.

Pollock, Lucy, Dr, *The Book About Getting Older (for people who don't want to talk about it)* (Michael Joseph, 2021)
This book features a range of very practical advice given by a doctor, herself bereaved of her husband, who has devoted her career to caring for older people. It is full of moving experiences with particular patients, their feelings and responses and the interchange between doctor and patient. How do we have conversations with those we love who are suffering the effects of age? With relationships at the core, this book really helps to start and develop that process.

Sagar, Leigh and Burroughs, Jack, *The Digital Estate, 2nd Edition* (Sweet & Maxwell, 2022)
A legal textbook covering digital assets from the perspective of fiduciaries such as personal representatives, trustees and attorneys. This includes cryptoassets, rights in cloud accounts, intellectual property and the digital records stored on computing devices. There is a discussion of the law relating to electronic documents and signatures. Legal analysis is combined with technical explanations, and the book offers practical advice, including a chapter on what to consider when drafting documents such as Wills.

Samuel, Julia, *Grief Works: Stories of Life, Death and Surviving* (Penguin Life, 2017)
A hugely powerful book written by grief psychotherapist Julia Samuel, with an extraordinary range of stories for those who have experienced loss – of a partner, parent, sibling or child. And then from people as they were facing their own death. There is a great intimacy in the book, which shows even how grief can bring healing, however extraordinary that might sound. So we can be helped, not only when we suffer bereavement ourselves, but also to support those close to us who suffer bereavement, through honest interaction and conversation.

Schultz, Patricia, *1,000 Places to See before You Die – a Traveller's Life List* **(Workman Publishing, 2012)**
This book is perfect for those who might have a 'bucket list' of places they want to see while able to go there. While, no doubt, updated research should be done before visiting, it is a really interesting and helpful guide before going on holiday – and also great for whetting the appetite.

Websites

Bereavement - www.AtaLoss.org
From the website: *"AtaLoss helps bereaved people to find support and wellbeing. Our vision is that no bereaved person in the UK should be left floundering or alone and unable to find support when they need it. We want there to be universal routine referrals so that everyone can find timely, appropriate and effective support in the interests of our mental and physical health as well as practical, financial, social and spiritual wellbeing."*

Bereavement - www.thebereavementjourney.org
From the website: *"Bereavement can impact hugely and affect all areas of life. Developed at Holy Trinity Brompton and appreciated by thousands of people over 20 years, The Bereavement Journey is for anyone who has been bereaved at any time and in any way. By means of a series of films and discussion groups, it gently guides bereaved people through the most common aspects of grief, enabling them to process the implications for themselves and discern next steps. Usually run by churches, The Bereavement Journey uniquely offers a final session on faith questions in bereavement provided from a Christian perspective. This is optional, thus making The Bereavement Journey suitable for people of any faith or none."*

Premium Bonds - www.nsandi.com/help/manage/money/form/others/customers/who/have/died
This National Savings & Investments website details the procedure to be followed and the options that are available following death.

Lasting Powers of Attorney - www.gov.uk/power-of-attorney
This is a Government website on how to make a Lasting Power of Attorney (LPA): starting an application online, choosing an attorney, certifying a copy and changing an LPA.

Organ Donation - www.organdonation.nhs.uk
This is an NHS website which sets out the facts about the organ donation process and deals with funeral arrangements, faith and beliefs, the opt-out system, family involvement and more.

Registering a Death - www.gov.uk/register-a-death
This is a Government website which tells you how to register a death in the UK or abroad, with content on finding a register office, applying for a certificate, correcting a registration, what to do after someone dies step-by-step and applying for probate.

Registering a Death - Tell Us Once
www.gov.uk/after-a-death/organisations-you-need-to-contact-and-tell-us-once
See page 70.

Resuscitation Council UK - www.respectprocess.org.uk
From the website: *"Resuscitation Council UK is saving lives by developing guidelines, influencing policy, delivering courses and supporting cutting-edge research. Through education, training and research, we are working towards the day when everyone in the country has the skills they need to save a life."* Among the content on the website is information on ReSPECT (Recommended Summary Plan for Emergency Care and Treatment), including a video which illustrates the process. See page 15.

ACKNOWLEDGEMENTS

Who to thank? First of all, Annie's and my daughter Alexandra for her unfailingly enthusiastic support of the project and for being my Marketing, Branding and Strategy Adviser.

Then, Annie, our daughter Victoria and son-in-law Matthew Doran and son David and daughter-in-law Liezl, all for their specific suggestions and general encouragement – and in the hope that my following my own advice will be a gift to them.

Third, my critical friends Christopher Compston, Jeremy Heal, Stephen Holt, Max Mackay-James and David Thompson for their painstaking reading of the text in draft and their various helpful observations and input.

Fourth, my PA Cheryl Gould for her both enthusiastic and careful transcription of recordings into text.

Fifth, Oliver Grant, for his imagination and artistic flair in producing the cartoons as illustrative of what the Book is trying to say.

Sixth, my editor Harriet Compston for her constant encouragement and her expert fine tuning of the text to ensure that it becomes the "easy and companionable read" which I hope that it is.

Seventh, Matt Day of Wetink for his brilliant design work and formatting of both the text and the Appendices to produce the printed Book and for his inspired creation of the Website, which is the key to the whole project.

Finally, for the section on Digital Assets in Chapter 1, I am indebted to the suggestions of Jack Burroughs of the Country Land and Business Association (whose book is referenced in Appendix 7 on page 97).

INDEX

ABOUT THE AUTHOR

Matthew was born and bred in Norfolk, growing up on the family farm. He studied classics at Oxford University and qualified as a solicitor in 1979. He practised first as a private client solicitor and then set up his own tax consultancy, advising, lecturing and writing books on estate planning and trusts, until his professional retirement in 2013. Since his father's death in 1984, he has been managing the farm. In 2014, he was ordained as a self-supporting minister in the Church of England. In 2020, Matthew was appointed a Deputy Lieutenant of the County of Norfolk. Married to Annie, they have three children and two grandchildren.